A Guide to
Child Protection Mediation
in
Ontario

By:
Paul James Brown

© 2017 Paul James Brown
paulbrownmediation.com
pauljamesbrown.com

All rights reserved. No part of this publication may be reproduced, stored in a retrieval system, or transmitted in any form by any process – electronic, mechanical, photocopying, recording, or otherwise – without the prior written permission of the author.

Printed in Canada and the United States of America by Lulu Press Inc.

ISBN 978-1-365-88930-1 (paperback)

paul@paulbrownmediation.com

This book dedicated to my beautiful wife, and amazing children for their endless patience and understanding. You push me to be the best person possible, and I'd be lost without you... PJB

Disclaimer:

The opinions expressed herein are those of the author, and do not necessary reflect those of the Government of Ontario, the Ministry of Children & Youth Services, Ontario Association of Children's Aid Societies, or the Ontario Association for Family Mediation.

Table of Contents

WHERE MY STORY STARTS 6
TERMINOLOGY 9
WHAT IS CHILD PROTECTION MEDIATION? 14
    FUNDING 16
HOW TO BECOME A CHILD PROTECTION MEDIATOR ..17
MINISTRY OF CHILDREN AND YOUTH SERVICES 19
WHAT IS THE CHILDREN'S AID SOCIETY 19
    CAS STRUCTURE 21
CHILD AND FAMILY SERVICES ACT 23
    DUTY TO REPORT 26
    ONTARIO RISK ASSESSMENT MODEL 28
    BILL 210 (Differential Response)..31
    ONTARIO REGULATION 496/ 06 32
    POLICY DIRECTIVE: CW 005-06......................................33
ELIGIBILITY SPECTRUM 35
THE PROCESS 37
REFERRAL 37
    CONSENT...38
    OFFICE OF THE CHILDREN'S LAWYER 39
INTAKE..41
    SCHEDULING..43
    CONFIDENTIALITY AGREEMENT................................44
    FAMILY MEMBER 48
    WORKER 59
    SAFE TERMINATION...63
VOICE OF THE CHILD 64
JOINT MEDIATION SESSION(S)...68
    AGREEMENT TO MEDIATE 71
    SHUTTLE MEDIATION...73
    SAFE TERMINATION..75
MEMORANDUM OF UNDERSTANDING 77
WHAT *NOT* TO DO..79
CONCLUSION...82
FUNCTIONAL DEFINITIONS OF MEDIATION 83

ARTICLES 85
  STICKS & STONES 85
  FILLING THE VOID..89
  THE FAMILY TRIANGLE 92
THANK YOU 96
APPENDIX..97
REFERENCES 110

WHERE MY STORY STARTS

My journey to becoming a mediator was anything but a direct path. The irony however is that as a young child, I always wanted to be a lawyer. Although I never made it to becoming a lawyer, I work hand-in-hand with them on an almost daily basis.

After high school, I fumbled from college program to college program (It is important to note that in Canada, College refers to Community College and University is what most Americans refer to as College). I started in Marketing Management, but I flunked out. Then I went to Pre-Health Sciences in hopes of becoming a Paramedic. It was next to impossible to get accepted into the Paramedic Program, so I enrolled in the Nursing Program. Again, I flunked out. I really had no idea what I was going to do, and doing security in a bar was not going to help me reach my future financial goals. Then it happened.

I was rolling with a friend in a Jiu-Jitsu class, and I got injured. Rolling is essentially a term for play-fighting on the ground in a martial arts class. Craig Connell had me in an arm bar, and I had a second to decide whether or not to tap (quit) or try and roll out. I chose the latter and ended up tearing the tendons at my elbow on the inside of my arm. As a result of the injury, I ended up in physiotherapy.

While in physiotherapy, I remembered thinking what a great job that would be. I was always fascinated by anatomy and physiology, and had worked out since I was a teenager. When I asked the therapist what training she had done, she told me she went to university but if she could do it again, she would have gone to college. I applied to George Brown College

(GBC) in Toronto Ontario Canada for the Fitness and Lifestyle Management Program, and was accepted.

Two years later, I graduated from the program, but always felt there was something missing. I had an excellent grasp on the physical body, but didn't know much about the mind. The program dealt a lot with anatomy, physiology, injury prevention, and exercise prescription, but there was little focus on the psychological or emotional wellness of our future clients. So, I graduated from GBC on a Friday in Spring 1998 and started my Psychology Degree at Trent University in Peterborough, Ontario on the Monday.

After graduating from GBC, I started working as a Personal Fitness Trainer and Group Exercise Instructor. I had a small client base, but I was able to pay my bills. I would also occasionally work with my father as an Iron Worker during shut-downs to make extra money. In June 2002, I began doing a shut-down, and was contemplating making a permanent move as an Iron Worker, because the money at that time was more consistent than as a small-time trainer. On July 22, 2002, everything would change.

At 11:20am, I was involved in a motorcycle accident. Someone made a left turn in front of me, and I t-boned their vehicle. My bike stopped immediately, however I flew over the car. I landed head first on the pavement on the other side of the car, and slid down the road. As a result of the accident, I was off work for over two years.

During the time I was off, I accelerated my psychology studies. Prior to the accident, I was attending school part-time. After the accident, I attended physiotherapy, massage therapy, and school. I also worked very hard at the gym to help with my rehabilitation.

Mediation is a mandatory step in the Accident Injury legal process in Ontario. For that process, I spent a day in Toronto Ontario with my lawyers, the insurance company's lawyer, a lawyer from the city in which the accident happened, and a mediator. We broke into separate rooms and when all was said and done, I only saw the mediator three times the whole day. I remember thinking that the mediator did very little that day. Then I got my bill and thought, THAT IS A GOOD JOB.

Shortly after that, I received a continuing education brochure from Trent U, and a mediation certificate was one of the options. I immediately signed up. There were two compulsory credits, and one elective credit necessary to receive the certificate. I chose Family Mediation as my elective.

In Fall 2004, I went back to work, and in December 2004, I began working in Group Homes. One year later, I began working at Hastings Children's Aid Society (HCAS) in Belleville Ontario Canada. Also in December 2005, I graduated from Trent University with an Honours Bachelor of Science Degree in Psychology.

I continued with my mediation studies while working at HCAS, because I knew I wouldn't be there long-term. I had tested and applied to be a firefighter, a police office, and even considered military service. On November 30, 2006, Bill 210 became law, and my life finally came into focus. I would become a Child Protection Mediator...

TERMINOLOGY

The following terms are used regularly in Child Protection Mediation, and are useful to know when facilitating this process. Terminology will be based on language of the Child Welfare system in the province of Ontario, Canada.

Child - any person under the age of eighteen (18).

Child In Need of Protection - a designation given to a child who MAY be at risk of physical and/ or emotional harm. In the legal system, only a judge may make an finding that a child is in need of protection under the Child and Family Services Act (CFSA). This finding is necessary before a judge may make an order under the CFSA.

Child Protection Worker - a Director, a local director or a person authorized by a Director or local director for the purposes of commencing child protection proceedings.

Children's Aid Society (CAS) or "Society" - an approved agency designated by the Minister of Children and Youth Services for a specified territorial jurisdiction, and for any or all of the functions set out in the Child & Family Services Act (CFSA).

Court - Ontario Court of Justice (OCJ) or the Family Branch of the Superior Court of Justice (SCJ). The CFSA is provincial legislation and as such, it is heard in the Ontario Court of Justice. In communities where an OCJ is not present, CFSA matters are heard in the Family Branch of the SCJ.

Crown Wardship - that the child be made a ward of the Crown (the State), until the wardship is terminated under section 65.2 of the CFSA or expires under subsection 71 (1) of the CFSA, and be placed in the care of the society. An order that the child be found in need of protection is required before a Crown Wardship order is made. The Crown becomes the child's permanent legal guardian.

Eligibility Spectrum - a tool designed to assist CAS staff in making consistent and accurate decisions about eligibility for service at the time of referral. The Eligibility Spectrum was most recently revised in 2016.

Kinship - a family member or close friend of the family. Typically used in reference to a placement outside of the family home, but not in foster care or a group care.

Parent - can be a biological parent, adoptive parent, someone who has lawful custody of the child, or an individual who has demonstrated an intention to treat the child as part of their family, or has acknowledged parentage of the child and provided for the child's support.

Place of Safety - a foster home, a hospital, a person's home that satisfies the requirements of CFSA Section 37 Subsection 5, or a place or one of a class of places designated as a place of safety by a Director or local director under section 18, but does not include,
    a) a place of secure custody as defined in Part IV, or
    b) a place of secure temporary detention as defined in Part IV

CFSA s.37 (5)

For the purposes of the definition of "place of safety" in subsection (1), a person's home is a place of safety for a child if,
    a) the person is a relative of the child or a member of the child's extended family or community; and
    b) a society or, in the case of a child who is an Indian or native person, an Indian or native child and family service authority designated under section 211 of Part X has conducted an assessment of the person's home in accordance with the prescribed procedures and is satisfied that the person is willing and able to provide a safe home environment for the child.

Plan of Care - a plan designed to meet a child's particular needs while in the care of the Society. It shall be prepared within thirty (30) days of the child's admission to the residential placement. The child has a right to participate in the development of their individual plan of care, and in any changes made to it.

Plan of Service - Used when the family is working voluntarily (ie not in court) with the CAS. A plan outlining how the CAS and family with work together for a specified period of time. It outlines tasks required of the CAS and family members.

Protection Application - a court application filed by CAS when the Society believes a child needs protection because of harm, or believes that a child is at risk of suffering harm. This is typically filed if the family is not willing to work with CAS voluntarily.

Referral - when someone contacts the local CAS to report concerns with respect to the well-being of a child.

Regulation - a rule or directive made and maintained by an authority designed to control or govern conduct. Compliance with regulations is mandatory.

Society Wardship - when a child is placed in the care and custody of the Society for a specified period not exceeding twelve (12) months. An order that the child be found in need of protection is required before a Society Wardship order is made. The Crown becomes the child's legal guardian for the duration of the order.

Standards - policies developed by the Ministry of Children and Youth Services as a means of directing and measuring specific program areas. Standards are mandatory, and establish a minimum level of performance to meet compliance requirements.

Supervision Order - when a child is placed in the care and custody of a parent or another person, subject to the supervision of the society, for a specified period of at least three (3) months and not more than twelve (12) months. An order that the child be found in need of protection is required before a Supervision Order is made.

Statute - provides overall direction and legal requirements that describe the official mandate and parameters of service delivery. For CAS, the key statute is the CFSA.

United Nations Convention on the Rights of the Child - a human rights treaty involving 196 countries, including Canada (1990) and the United States of America (1995). The convention sets out civil, political, economic, social, health, and cultural rights of children. The convention defines a child as "any human being under the age of eighteen (18), unless the age of majority is attained earlier under national legislation."

WHAT IS CHILD PROTECTION MEDIATION?

Alternative Dispute Resolution (ADR) processes are typically considered as an alternative to litigation. In Ontario Canada, the prescribed methods of Child Welfare ADR include Child Protection Mediation, Family Group Conferencing (also referred to as Family Group Decision-Making in Ontario), and various Native processes. There are other forms of ADR that have been approved by the Ministry of Children and Youth Services (MCYS), however those methods are used on a smaller scale in individual communities. For the purposes of this text, the term ADR will refer exclusively to Child Protection Mediation, Family Group Conferencing/ Family Group Decision-Making, and approved Native methods.

Child Protection Mediation (CP Med) is a specialized form of Family Mediation, and follows many of the same principles. It is a voluntary process involving family members, a representative from CAS, and sometimes a lawyer appointed by the Office of the Children's Lawyer. It is a process wherein a family, CAS worker, and when assigned, a lawyer for the child work together to plan for the well-being of the child. It is facilitated by a specially trained, impartial facilitator who has no decision making authority. The overarching purpose of CP Med is to help the parties come to an agreement that addresses the identified child protection concerns.

CP Med is emotional work. The families involved may have had their children removed from their care, or may be facing that possibility if their situation does not change. They may be involved in a complex legal battle with CAS, and have an overwhelming sense of powerlessness. Many of the clients involved in the child welfare system are underprivileged, feel marginalized, and often feel unheard. For these reasons, it is incredibly important that the facilitator be well-versed in mediation strategies, and have an open mind for the population with whom they work.

The purpose of CP Med is not to determine if a child is in need of protection. When CAS opens a file, they do so because they believe that there is a child in need of protection. From a legal perspective, only a judge may make a "finding" that a child is need of protection. A "finding" must be in place prior to a judge making an order in Child Welfare court.

Child Welfare ADR was added to Child and Family Services Act (CFSA) to assist families and CAS' with working through a plethora of issues. CP Med is only one method available, and may be used to explore solutions to almost any issue in a child protection case. The intent was to help families and CAS' work more cooperatively. Unfortunately, CAS' have come to view CP Med as a means to assist only families engaged in custody and access disputes. Although not traditional child protection cases, these files can often have levels of conflict that quickly put the child at risk of harm. As a result, CAS intervenes and often makes a referral to CP Med.

Recently, a shift has started to take place wherein CAS is also making referrals for other types of cases. Although not an exhaustive list, some examples of possible CP Med referrals include:

- Custody and Access
- Customary Care Arrangements
- Family Communication
- Terms of CAS Involvement/ Plan of Service Tasks
- File transfer from another agency
- Adoption Openness
- Parent-Teen Conflict
- Reintegration Strategies

FUNDING

The ADR process is funded by MCYS, and funneled to facilitators by a Transfer Payment Agency (TPA). MCYS also funds the CAS agencies in the province, however the facilitators are not paid by the CAS. Most facilitators in the province are private clinicians. In an effort to remain neutral and transparent, mediators should ensure that clients are aware that the funding for CP Med and CAS comes from the same Ministry, however the mediator is not paid by CAS.

HOW TO BECOME A CHILD PROTECTION MEDIATOR

In order to do CP Med work in the province of Ontario, mediators must be on the Ontario Child Protection Mediation Roster. The roster is currently managed by Ontario Association for Family Mediation (OAFM) on behalf of MCYS. Interested mediators must complete a five (5) day course in order to be listed on the roster. To register for the course, candidates must meet the following criteria:

1. Accreditation as a Family Mediator (OAFM), Certification as a Family Mediator (Family Mediation Canada), or Chartered status as a Family Mediator (Alternative Dispute Resolution Institute of Ontario), or equivalency, defined as:
  a) A professional degree or diploma in the social services or children's services;
  b) Completion of at least 60 hours of training in family mediation, to include 20 hours of skill based training;
  c) Completion of 14 hours of domestic violence training;
  d) Completion of at least 10 family law mediation cases to the point of agreement, with submission of Memorandum of Understanding.

2. Proof of professional liability insurance.

3. A satisfactory criminal record check or submission of your security clearance number, both obtained within the last three (3) years.

4. Three (3) satisfactory professional references, two (2) of which must be from people with whom you have co-mediated a family matter or who have referred family law cases to you.

5. Signed declaration form to abide by the OAFM CP Med Code of Professional Conduct.

6. A current curriculum vitae.

The five (5) day CP Med course is an evaluated course. Participants must successfully pass the written test as well as evaluated role play exercises. Upon successful completion, candidates will be added to the Ontario Provincial Mediation Roster. Once a mediator is on the provincial roster, they may then attempt to have their name added to sub-rosters held by the local TPA's. CP Mediators should be aware that being accepted on the provincial roster does not guarantee acceptance on a TPA's sub-roster, nor does it guarantee cases will be assigned.

MINISTRY OF CHILDREN AND YOUTH SERVICES

In 2003, the Ministry of Children and Youth Services (MCYS) was created to coordinate services for families and children. The Ministry's overarching goals are to:
- make it easier for families to find the services they need to give children the best start in life,
- make it easier for families to access the services they need at all stages of a child's development,
- help youth to become productive adults

MCYS administers the CFSA with the exception of Sections 162 - 174 inclusive. Sections 162 to 174 of the Child and Family Services Act relate specifically to adoption records.

WHAT IS THE CHILDREN'S AID SOCIETY

The Children's Aid Society (CAS) is a "non-government organization." Although they are funded by MCYS, they are independent from the government of Ontario. CAS is dedicated to ensuring the protection and well-being of children in the province. In the United States, a comparable term is Child Protective Services.

Currently (2017), there are forty-four (44) CAS agencies, and four (4) Aboriginal CAS agencies in Ontario. In recent years, there have been amalgamations to decrease the number of CAS agencies in the province, and it is generally understood that there will be more amalgamations to further reduce that number. All of these agencies belong to a larger organization known as the Ontario Association of Children's Aid Societies (OACAS). OACAS has been around since 1920, and is responsible for advocacy, government relations, public education, and training. OACAS is governed by a voluntary Board of Directors.

Section 15 of the CFSA describes the functions of CAS as:

a) investigate allegations or evidence that children who are under the age of sixteen (16) years or are in the society's care or under its supervision may be in need of protection
b) protect, where necessary, children who are under the age of sixteen (16) years or are in the society's care or under its supervision
c) provide guidance, counselling and other services to families for protecting children or for the prevention of circumstances requiring the protection of children
d) provide care for children assigned or committed to its care under this Act

e) supervise children assigned to its supervision under this Act
f) place children for adoption under Part VII; and,
g) perform any other duties given to it by this or any other Act.

CAS STRUCTURE

The hierarchy of CAS starts with front-line workers. Front-line workers report to supervisors, who report to managers. Managers report to the Director(s) of Service, who then reports to the Executive Director. The Executive Director is primarily a political position, and they report to a volunteer Board of Directors.

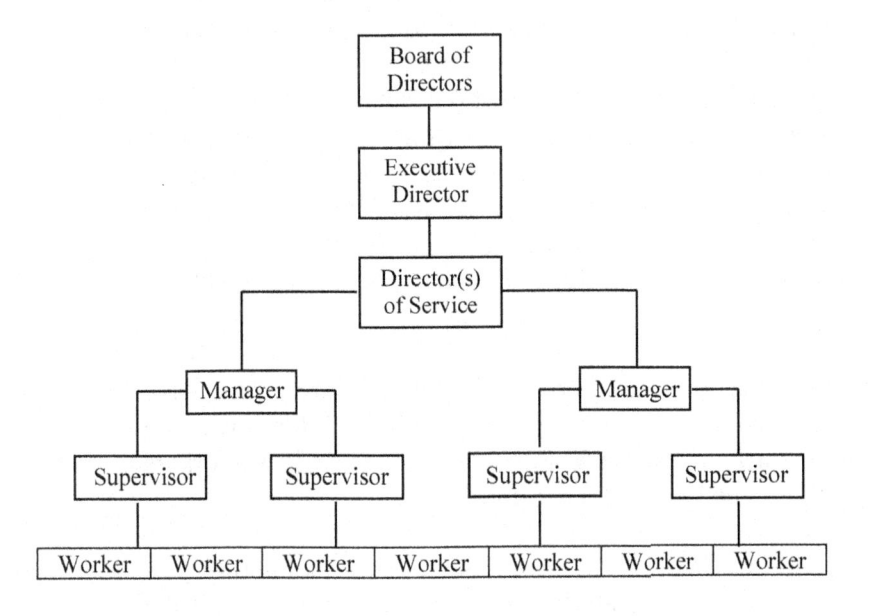

```
                    Board of Directors
                           |
                    Executive Director
                           |
                    Director(s) of Service
                    /                  \
               Manager               Manager
              /      \              /       \
       Supervisor  Supervisor  Supervisor  Supervisor
         /  \        /  \        /   \       /   \
    Worker Worker Worker Worker Worker Worker Worker Worker
```

In CP Med, mediators primarily deal with front-line workers and sometimes, supervisors. Front-line workers include but are not limited to Child Protections Workers (often referred to as Family Services Workers or simply "Workers"), Children's Services Workers, Adoption Workers and sometimes, Resource Workers. In some agencies, Family Services Workers are divided into Intake Workers (handle the investigations), and Ongoing Workers (work with the family long-term). In other agencies, they are occasionally referred to as Generic Workers as they handle both Intake and Ongoing cases. Family Services Workers are the case managers of the protection file.

At this time, Child Protection Workers are neither required to be Social Workers, nor do they have to be registered with the *Ontario College of Social Workers and Social Service Workers*. There is speculation that this will change, however it is not currently in place. Child Protection Workers are tasked with doing Child Protection work; not social work. They often have varied degrees and education such as Psychology, Criminology, Sociology etc, and all Child Protection Workers must complete New Worker Training prior to becoming an authorized worker. This training is also under review, and it is anticipated that workers will require certification to practice Child Protection after having achieved a set level of competency.

Children's Services Workers work with children who have been admitted to CAS care. This may include children who are Society Wards or Crown Wards. Children's Services Workers are just that; the worker for the child.

An Adoption Worker is responsible for facilitating the adoption process for both the family that is adopting and the child who is being adopted. Adoption workers often use mediation to discuss openness with respect to children and birth families. Especially important in this technologically modern world, there is a high probability that adoptive children will use technology to seek out their birth family later in life. It is better to discuss some planning for that well in advance.

Resource Workers are responsible for finding placements for children who are admitted to CAS care. They are also responsible for assessing potential foster placements, and kinship homes. Kinship placements are often used as an alternative to admitting a child into CAS care. The goal of kinship placements is to better support family relationships. It is also more cost effective for CAS to support in-family placements than it is to admit a child into CAS care.

Most kinship placements are voluntary, and do not require court intervention. For a child to be admitted to CAS care, the matter has to be heard in court. If a child is apprehended, CAS must bring the matter to court within five (5) days of the child being admitted to CAS care. The exception would be if there is a voluntary Temporary Care Agreement between the parents and the CAS in which case, court is not necessary.

CHILD AND FAMILY SERVICES ACT

In Ontario Canada, the Child and Family Services Act (CFSA) is the legislation that governs all Children's Aid Societies in the province. They are the rules under which the CAS operates. When I meet with clients, I describe the CFSA as the rules of the CAS; much like the Highway Traffic Act contains the rule of the roads.

The main purpose of the CFSA is to "promote the best interests, protection and well-being of children." It emphasizes that CAS interventions should be from least intrusive to most intrusive and ideally, on mutual consent of the family and CAS. The Act also stresses that services to families should be respectful of the family's cultural, religious, and regional differences.

The section of the CFSA that directly relates to ADR is Section 20.2. Section 20.2 (1) states:

If a child is or may be in need of protection under this Act, a society shall consider whether a prescribed method of alternative dispute resolution could assist in resolving any issue related to the child or a plan for the child's care.

This is important as it implies that in every file that is open to CAS for protection services, CAS must consider ADR. To be clear, the Act does not say that ADR must occur with every file, but ADR must be considered. If a file closes without ADR being considered, CAS has not met their criteria as set out in the legislation.

Section 20.2 (2) states:

If the issue referred to in subsection (1) relates to a child who is an Indian or native person, the society shall consult with the child's band or native community to determine whether an alternative dispute resolution process established by that band or native community or another prescribed process will assist in resolving the issue.

With respect to children who are Indian or Native, they are entitled to receive services that include their specific traditions. The Act highlights that the child's band or native community will be contacted, to enquire if the band/community has their own form of dispute resolution services. With this information, CAS will discuss different methods, including Native approaches of ADR with the family. It is then the family's choice as to the form of ADR in which they would like to participate. There are also circumstances when approaches will be blended to better fit the needs of the individual family.

Section 20.2 (3) states:

If a society or a person, including a child, who is receiving child welfare services proposes that a prescribed method of alternative dispute resolution be undertaken to assist in resolving an issue relating to a child or a plan for the child's care, the Children's Lawyer may provide legal representation to the child if in the opinion of the Children's Lawyer such legal representation is appropriate.

When a referral is made for ADR, a referral is also sent to the Office of the Children's Lawyer (OCL) in Toronto, Ontario. A representative from the OCL will then determine if a lawyer will be appointed to represent the child in the ADR process. This will be discussed in more detail in "The Process" section.

Section 20.2 (4) states:

If a society makes or receives a proposal that a prescribed method of alternative dispute resolution be undertaken under subsection (3) in a matter involving a child who is an Indian or native person, the society shall give the child's band or native community notice of the proposal.

If the ADR process has begun for a child who is Indian or Native, the Society must notify the child's band or native community. The band may then reach out to the family to provide additional support to the family if the family consents.

DUTY TO REPORT

Section 72 of the CFSA relates to duty to report. Duty to report is a person's responsibility to notify the local CAS if they believe a child is at risk of harm. The CFSA says "if a person, including a person who performs professional or official duties with respect to children..." The CFSA goes a step further, and lists specific professionals. In fact, Section 72(5)(b.2) specifically references mediators as having a duty to report if they have reasonable belief that a child is at risk of harm. Although the CFSA highlights professionals as having a responsibility, they are included in the larger group of citizens. As such, every person (with the exception of solicitor-client privilege) has an obligation to report if they honestly believe a child is at risk of harm.

This section of the CFSA supersedes any other act. That is to say that there is no legal reason that a person can refuse to report if they believe a child is in need of protection. If a person knowingly does not report concerns that a child may be in need of protection, they may be charged. If convicted, they face the possibility of a fine and/ or imprisonment.

If a person believes that a child may be in need of protection, it is that person's responsibility to provide the local CAS with the information. The person receiving the information firsthand must make the referral; not someone else within their agency. For example, if a teacher receives information that a child may be at risk of harm, it is the teacher who must make the referral; not the school principal.

Reasons to make a referral, and why CAS may become involved with a family include but are not limited to:
- physical harm or risk of physical harm inflicted by a caregiver or as a result of lack of supervision or neglect
- sexual assault/ exploitation (including child pornography) or risk of sexual assault/ exploitation (including child pornography) by a caregiver or by someone else and the caregiver fails to protect the child
- failure to provide for the child's medical needs
- emotional harm demonstrated by serious anxiety, depression, withdrawal, self-destructive/ aggressive behaviour or delayed development, and there are reasonable grounds to believe the emotional harm is a result of actions or failure to act by the caregiver.
- emotional harm or risk of emotional harm noted above and the caregiver does not provide or consent to services to alleviate the harm.
- the child suffers from a mental, emotional or development condition that if not remedied, could seriously impair their development and the caregiver does not provide or does not/ cannot consent to treatment to alleviate the condition.

- child has been abandoned either by choice or by caregiver death
- child is younger than twelve (12), and has killed or seriously injured a person or caused serious damage to another person's property, AND the caregiver refuses or is unable to consent to treatment services.
- child is younger than twelve (12) and on more than one occasion injured another person or caused damage to another person's property with the encouragement of the caregiver or due to lack of supervision.

When making a referral to CAS, some people fear retaliation. From a legal perspective, there will be no action against a person who makes a referral to CAS in good faith. Also, employers are not permitted to discipline staff in any way for having made a referral to CAS. The Act also allows for the protection of a referents identity. The identity of the referent cannot be released to the identified family or to the person believed to have caused the child to be in need of protection unless required or permitted in a court proceeding.

ONTARIO RISK ASSESSMENT MODEL

In 1997, a decision was made to implement a common risk assessment tool across Ontario. The Ontario Risk Assessment Model (ORAM) was designed as a standardized, comprehensive approach to the assessment of risk across all CAS agencies. ORAM's primary goal was to promote and support a structured and rational decision-making approach to case practice, without replacing professional judgement. The specific tools included in ORAM were intended to help workers design strategies to reduce risk, and build on family strengths.

ORAM had seven (7) key components:

1. Eleven Risk Decision Points
  i. Does the case meet eligibility requirements for child welfare services?
  ii. What is the response time?
  iii. Is the child safe now?
  iv. Are the child protection concerns verified?
  v. Is the child in need of protection?
  vi. Is the child at risk of future abuse or neglect?
  vii. What other assessment issues must be considered to inform the plan of service?
  viii. What is the plan of service for the child and family?
  ix. Does the case continue to meet eligibility requirements for child protection service?
  x. Have assessments changed?
  xi. Should the plan of service be modified?

2. Standards to Guide Each Decision Point

These were new standards for each risk decision, and were designed to provide support and consistency for decisions made for each child protection case.

3. Eligibility Assessment

Child protection staff use the *Eligibility Spectrum* at the time of the referral to make decisions about the eligibility for service. The *Eligibility Spectrum* helps CAS staff to consistently interpret the need for child protection intervention.

The *Eligibility Spectrum* is still in use today.

4. Safety Assessment and Immediate Planning

The child protection worker completes the *Safety Assessment* at the first face-to-face contact with a child following a new or subsequent referral that requires investigation. When immediate safety interventions are required to ensure the child's safety while the investigation continues, an *Immediate Safety Intervention Plan* is completed.

5. Risk Assessment

The child protection worker uses their knowledge of Risk Assessment during the investigation phase and on an ongoing basis to assess the likelihood of future harm to the child. The child protection worker completes the *Risk Assessment Tool* when the assessment determines that a child is in need of protection and for subsequent case reviews.

6. Assessment of Other Child Protection Issues

The child protection worker completes an assessment of child protection issues to ensure that all issues related to the child's best interests, protection and well-being are addressed. It includes such subject areas as child development, and long-term parenting capacity.

7. Plan of Service Connected to the Risk Assessment of Other Child Protection Issues

The child protection worker, while completing the Risk Assessment and the assessment of other child protection issues, and involving relevant parties, identifies issues to be addressed in the Plan of Service. The child protection worker determines outcomes required to reduce risk and the child's need for protection, and establishes strategies for achieving those outcomes. In this way, the information from the investigation and assessment process is linked directly to the planned interventions contained in the Plan of Service.

Although ORAM is no longer practiced, there are elements of the model that remain in use today including but not limited to:

- Eligibility Spectrum (updated)
- Safety Assessment (updated/ redesigned)
- Risk Assessment (updated/ redesigned)

BILL 210 (Differential Response)

On November 30, 2006, Bill 210 rolled out in Ontario Canada, and included several significant amendments to the CFSA. Other names used to reference the Bill were *Transformation Agenda*, and *Differential Response* (DR). Bill 210 aimed to achieve better outcomes for children and youth while promoting their safety, well-being, and permanency. The changes in CAS service delivery were designed to create:

- A more flexible and responsive intake and assessment model.
- A court process strategy to help reduce delays for children and youth and to promote alternatives to court through alternate dispute resolution methods
- A broader range of placement and intervention options to support early and effective permanency planning.

DR is a way of delivering child welfares services that allows greater flexibility than ORAM in the approach to child safety.

DR is meant to be adaptable based on the presenting issues and needs, while still keeping the safety of the child at the forefront.

One of the big changes associated with DR was involving families more in the decision-making process, and encouraging a strengths-based approach to working with them. To be clear, DR was not implemented to forget about risk. It was introduced as a means to empower families and reduce risk. Part of the empowerment came from introducing ADR into the legislation.

ONTARIO REGULATION 496/ 06

This Regulation outlines criteria of the ADR process, but does not specifically list the prescribed processes. It indicates that the prescribed method of ADR must meet the following criteria:
- entered into with consent of all participants
- the process can be terminated at any time by any of the participants
- conducted by an impartial facilitator with no decision-making authority
- must satisfy the Regulation's confidentiality requirements
- must not be an arbitration.

The confidentiality provisions of this Regulation are:

- nobody involved in the ADR process, including the facilitator can be asked to give evidence or produce documents in a civil proceeding about anything to do with the ADR process.

Note: Family court and court involving CAS are both considered civil court.

- none of the content of the ADR meetings is admissible in civil court:
    → unless there are reasonable grounds to believe that someone may be at risk of harm (including Duty to Report if a child may be in need of protection).
    → unless an individual consents to the disclosure of their own personal information
    → the terms of an agreement, memorandum of understanding or plan arising out of the ADR may be shared with the court, and all lawyers for the participants
- the ADR facilitator may disclose non-identifying information for research or educational purposes, but the facilitator must inform the parties of this possibility prior to the ADR process beginning.
- the participants may discuss the content of ADR with their lawyer.

Many of the Agreements to Mediate in circulation today, have these confidentiality provisions built in to ensure that the participants are made aware in advance of the joint mediation session.

POLICY DIRECTIVE: CW 005-06

The MCYS issued this Policy Directive effective November 30, 2006; the same day that Bill 210 came into law. There is currently a group working with MCYS to discuss changes to this directive however, no formal changes have been implemented as of yet.

There is considerable overlap among contents of this Directive, Ontario Regulation 496/ 06, and the CFSA. In this Directive however, there are key points not made elsewhere. This Directive specifically mentions the three (3) prescribed forms of ADR to be used under the CFSA, facilitator qualification criteria and impartiality, CAS record keeping with respect to ADR, and more.

CP Med is a closed process. That is to say that aside from the mediated agreement, none of the information from the process is made available outside of the meeting(s). CAS does however have specific obligations with respect to their reporting of CP Med. CAS is required to consider ADR in every case and once considered, they must keep a record of that consideration, and reasons they decided to move forward with ADR or not move forward with ADR. CAS must also track outcomes of the ADR process, and report back to MCYS on a quarterly basis.

FACILITATOR IMPARTIALITY

Ontario Regulation 496/ 06 requires ADR facilitators to be impartial, and have no decision-making authority. This policy further defines impartiality. There is also clarification as to when facilitators are also employed by a CAS.

When possible, the facilitator should be employed outside of a CAS; whether it be self-employment or through a different agency. When employed by a CAS, facilitators SHOULD have their own office, and when possible, have their ADR meetings at a location outside of CAS. If employed by a CAS, facilitators MUST:
- have a distinct role separate from the child protection role and the child welfare team

- not have access to client files or CAS database
- not have access to casenotes or court information
- not report to a child protection supervisor, and must report to senior management

ELIGIBILITY SPECTRUM

The *Eligibility Spectrum* is a tool designed to assist CAS staff in making consistent and accurate decisions about a family's eligibility for service at the time of referral. When CAS receives information about a child, the Eligibility Spectrum is used to code the referral based on the reason for service/ allegations, the level of severity, and response time. The referral coding can be deviated provided there is a reasonable explanation documented in the CAS file.

Referrals to the CAS are coded according to the following sections:

1. Physical/Sexual Harm by Commission
2. Harm By Omission
3. Emotional Harm
4. Abandonment/Separation
5. Caregiver Capacity
6. Request for Counselling
7. Request for Adoption Services
8. Family Based Care
9. Volunteer Services
10. Request for Assistance
11. Request for Youth Services

If the referral codes in Section one (1) to eight (8), it is then further scaled numerically. The second number is a more specific sub-category of the type of alleged maltreatment. Referrals are then given a letter designation to indicate the level of severity. The level of severity is what determines the response time. Referrals are coded as either a twelve (12) hour response, a seven (7) day response, or not response at all.

THE PROCESS

REFERRAL

Anyone may suggest ADR on an open CAS file, however the referral process is initiated by the assigned worker. It is the local TPA that sets the referral process, and the referral is filtered through them in some way. The referral process varies from location to location. For example, the referral process in Toronto Ontario is very different than the referral process in Peterborough, Ontario.

Some CAS' send the referral to the local TPA who then assigns the case to a mediator. That mediator may be selected as they are next on the roster to receive a case, or they may have been requested to be the mediator. Other CAS' send the referral directly to the mediator. In some instances, the worker must get approval from the local TPA prior to proceeding with the mediation referral. They are then required to find their own CP mediator.

There is also variation in the referral form. Some TPA's ask the worker to fill out a specific referral form. Others use the Office of the Children's Lawyer Notice of ADR referral form. In some areas, the worker only needs to phone the mediator to initiate the process. If you are considering CP Med as a practice, be sure to check with the local TPA for their policies and processes, and make sure you are able to practice on their roster before accepting a CP Med file.

CONSENT

Prior to initiating the ADR referral, the worker must have consent of the parties. This is not a mandatory requirement of the mediation process per se, but it is a requirement of the

Freedom of Information and Protection of Privacy Act. Without the consent of the participants, the CAS should not be disclosing any identifiable information about the participants. It is very frustrating to call a client to initiate an intake appointment, only to find out they have no idea that a mediation referral has been made.

Ideally, CAS should ask the family member to sign a consent form like the example in *Appendix A*. Although verbal consent is sufficient, best practice is to have a signed consent form. The form can then be uploaded to the file, to confirm that the participant consented. This is important for the worker if the file is ever audited. It is also a clear indication that ADR was considered on the file. Depending on the TPA and/ or the mediator, sometimes the signed consent form will be included with the CP Med referral.

OFFICE OF THE CHILDREN'S LAWYER

The Office of the Children's Lawyer (OCL) is a division of the Ministry of the Attorney General (MAG). The OCL represents children under the age of eighteen (18) in court cases involving custody and access and child protection. They will also represent children in civil, and estates and trusts cases. The OCL employs both lawyers and clinicians (typically social workers), who work on a fee-for-service basis across the province.

As per Policy Directive CW 005-06, CAS must notify the OCL when they make a referral for ADR. If a lawyer is not currently involved to represent the child, CAS is required to use the prescribed referral form as shown in *Appendix B*. After reviewing the OCL Referral form, the OCL will then decide whether or not to appoint a lawyer for the child with respect to the ADR. It is not uncommon for a representative from the OCL to consult with the worker and/ or the mediator in making that determination. Once a determination is made, a representative from the OCL will notify the worker of the decision and oftentimes, the mediator as well.

There are also instances when a lawyer has already been appointed to represent the child. This typically occurs when a protection case is before the court, and a lawyer has been appointed to represent the child in that forum. If that is the case, the worker has an obligation to inform the assigned children's lawyer that the referral for mediation has been submitted. It is not necessary for the worker to send the prescribed Notice of ADR to the OCL in these instances.

Note: If a lawyer is representing a child in court, discussion needs to happen with the lawyer before the ADR referral is submitted to ensure that the lawyer (and their client) consent to the process being initiated; much like the adult parties.

When meeting with the family to discuss CP Med and ask for consent, the worker should inform the family that a referral will also be made to the OCL as part of the process.

There is some confusion as to which types of CP Med cases require OCL notification. At this time, the short answer is all of them. It does not matter the child's age, type of case, or whether or not there is court involvement. The OCL must be made aware of CP Med referrals. If the mediator receives a CP Med referral in which an OCL referral has not been made, the mediator should direct the worker to notify the OCL as soon as possible; whether it be completing the prescribed form or contacting a lawyer already assigned to represent the child.

As noted earlier, there is currently a working group reviewing Policy Directive CW 005-06. As part of that process, the OCL notification requirements are being reviewed, and it is possible that some changes to the notification process will result.

INTAKE

When ADR first rolled out in 2006, the expectation was that none of the mediation appointments be held at the CAS office. The worry about having appointments at the CAS office was the perception that the mediator may be aligned with the CAS and as a result, not impartial. The thinking around this issue has evolved over time.

Many clients found that meeting at a different location actually created increased stress for them. When meeting at CAS, they know where the office is, and already have experience with finding transportation to that location. So in some instances, meeting at the CAS office can actually reduce potential stress. As mediators, our role is to help families; not create added stress.

Currently, many mediators facilitate CP Med at the CAS office. As mentioned above, this can be more convenient for participants. Also, some mediators service multiple communities, and renting several offices in not financially feasible. If mediators are holding meetings with family members at CAS offices, mediators need to inform participants that CAS is only being used as a result of space availability and not because of any alliance with CAS. Further, if a participant is not comfortable meeting at the CAS office, the mediator needs to make arrangements to meet the participants elsewhere.

Other possible meeting locations include but are not limited to churches, libraries, lawyer's office, and other professional office space. Occasionally, participants will ask to meet at a local restaurant. A public location like a restaurant is not ideal due to the confidential and emotional nature of the conversation. If the clients insists however, an intake appointment could be held in a public setting. There are even instances when intake appointments could be facilitated outside. Ultimately, the goal is to make the participant feel comfortable with the process, gain their trust, and gather the necessary information required to determine if the mediation will proceed.

It is not uncommon for participants to ask to meet in their home. In Family Group Conferencing/ Decision-Making, the expectation is that the facilitator meet with the family members in their home or a location of their choosing. Prior to client contact however, the facilitator has met with the CAS, and has an understanding of the family dynamics and who the participants are. From that information, they are able to make important decisions about where to meet participants, and ensure facilitator safety. If the client is the first person you are meeting, meeting in their home is strongly discouraged as there is insufficient information to ensure your safety.

SCHEDULING

It is important to maintain neutrality throughout the entire mediation process. Because the referral comes from the worker, they are usually the first point of contact. As a result, their intake appointment is often scheduled first. To be clear, this does not always mean that the worker is the first person seen. It simply means they are *often* the first person contacted. As a general rule, I contact the participants in the order in which their contact information is listed on the referral. All appointments are based strictly on calendar availability. The order in which intakes are completed should not matter.

There are some mediators who believe that they should meet with the worker first. I disagree. If the default is to meet with the worker first, the perception to clients may be that the CAS' information is the most important information for the mediator to receive. Some mediators believe they should meet with the worker first so the mediator may share why CAS is involved or why CAS believes mediation would be helpful. Again, I disagree with this. It is neither the mediator's role nor their responsibility to share that information. It is the worker's! All intake appointments must be treated as confidential. It is the same concept as a family mediation. A mediator should not disclose any content from the other client's intake appointment. In CP Med, a worker is a client; just as a family member is a client.

The Ontario CP Med Manual (2006) states that family members should be met before CAS workers. Again, I disagree. The reason it is recommended to meet with family members first is because of the inherent power imbalance that exists between CAS and family members. Although there may be a perceived power differential between CAS and a family, there are many dynamics to consider when assessing power. This may include experience of the worker, strength of individual personalities, or merits of the child protection case. Another point to consider is which of the family members are met first, because there are often several family members involved.

It is important that all parties, including CAS see the mediator as neutral and impartial. Strategically meeting with a certain person first has the potential to create a perceived bias. Actual bias is not as important as perceived bias. How clients perceive the mediator and the process will dictate how they interact with the mediator and the process.

YOUR PERCEPTION IS EQUAL TO YOUR REALITY

CONFIDENTIALITY AGREEMENT

As discussed, CP Med is covered by the regulations, policy directives, and legislation associated with the CFSA. Many of our clients however, are not aware of this information. As a means of sharing this necessary information, I ask clients to sign a confidentiality agreement at the beginning of their intake appointment. I use this document as a tool for explaining the process. It helps set the tone for the meetings, and lets people know that their information is safe with the mediator.

Appendix C shows a standard Confidentiality Agreement. Below is a breakdown of the document, and an explanation of what is included:

1. *Mediation is a voluntary process, and any participant has the right to withdraw from the process at any time.*

It is important to inform clients that the process is voluntary. Many clients attend mediation thinking it is a mandatory process in which they must engage. When asked what they would like to get out of mediation, it is not uncommon to hear "CAS told me I have to come." Even though the worker may have only suggested ADR, because the suggestion came from CAS, clients often feel it is mandatory. The same can be said about judges making the "suggestion."

2. *The mediator was an employee of the Hastings Children's Aid Society until July 4, 2011. The mediator is no longer an employee of the Hastings Children's Aid Society and as such, does not have access to the family's child welfare history beyond what is disclosed in the mediation process.*

As someone who once worked as a Child Protection Worker, I am very aware that not all clients like CAS. There are also those who believe that the system is stacked against them. It is very important for me that I inform clients of any potential conflicts of interests right away. I also use this as an opportunity to inform them that I know the child welfare system, and may be able to take time to explain why certain events happen when working with CAS. Clients appreciate the honesty. I have conducted hundreds of child welfare mediations, and have not had a client refuse service yet as a result of my CAS background.

3. *The mediator will not voluntarily disclose any verbal and/ or written communication that takes place during this meeting. The following exceptions apply:*
- *Disclosure for my lawyer or third party advisors;*
- *Where information suggests an actual or perceived threat to human life and/ or safety (notify CAS for a child, notify Police for an adult);*
- *Where ordered to do so by law;*
- *Research and/ or educational purposes (non-identifying information);*
- *On written consent*

These are standard confidentiality clauses, but it is important to ensure that clients know where their information will and will not go. Further, these are items included in Section 2 of Ontario Regulation 496/ 06.

4. *I consent to the presence of language interpreters, mediation interns and/ or assistants for the purposes of professional training. All such observers and/ or participants are also bound by the same rules of confidentiality as the mediator as outlined in Paragraph 3.*

When working in larger, more culturally diverse communities, it is not uncommon for interpreters to be present for meetings. Also, many mediators have observers and interns connected with their practice. It is important for clients to understand that other individuals in the meeting must also keep the information confidential.

5. *I shall not record the content of any mediation appointments through any means such as audio, video etc.*

In my years as a protection worker, I had several clients record conversations. As a result, there remains worry that conversations may be recorded in the child welfare mediation process. If I become aware that a client is recording our conversations and/ or meetings, I will terminate the meeting. There is only one (1) reason a client would record a conversation, and that is to use it as evidence in the future. Child Protection Mediation is a closed process and as such, none of the information, aside from the Memorandum of Understanding is to be used in any future civil proceeding.

I also use this as an opportunity to inform workers and clients that only the mediator may take notes during the joint mediation session(s). This will be covered in further detail in the Joint Mediation Session section.

6. *I shall not summons nor otherwise require the mediator to testify and/or produce records and/ or notes in any current or future civil proceedings.*

This informs people that information shared with the mediator is not going to make its way into any court documents.

I acknowledge that I have read the Confidentiality Agreement or had it read to me, and understand this agreement.

Many of the clients I work with have literacy challenges. This may be a result of education, trauma, or developmental challenges. Regardless of the reason, it exists. As a result, I read all documents to my clients, and explain each paragraph in everyday language. This way, I believe the information is understood, and the client does not feel marginalized due to possible literacy challenges. Policy Directive CW 005-06 indicates that:

"a written confidentiality agreement could act as a disincentive to certain persons to engaging in a prescribed method of ADR. In these cases, the minimum expectation is that children's aid societies only engage in a prescribed method of ADR where the elements of the confidentiality regulation are clearly communicated to participants by the ADR facilitator at the outset of the process."

By explaining the content of the agreement(s) with the clients, including the confidentiality clauses, the participants are still entering into an approved form of child welfare ADR.

FAMILY MEMBER

Everything we talk about today is completely confidential, and just between you and me. Exceptions to that would be if I think someone is at risk of harm. Then I have to report it. So, if I think you are going to hurt yourself or someone else, I need to make a phone call.

I also make sure that everyone I work with knows that I used to be a CAS Worker. I'm not anymore, and haven't been for about _____ years, but I like to make sure everyone knows where I came from. If it's an issue, we can talk about it. If not, we'll just keep going.

This is a pretty standard introduction that I use at the beginning of an intake appointment with family members. I immediately highlight confidentiality, duty to report, and potential conflict of interest. My hope is that by covering these details in the introduction, I avoid any surprises or misunderstandings of my role later in the meeting. Clients often want to start telling their story right away, but it is important to explain duty to report obligations before receiving any personal information.

After the mediator introduces themselves, it is important to explain the process to the participant. Clients need to be made aware that just because they want to do mediation does not mean it will proceed. Part of the intake process is screening to ensure that the people and the case dynamics are appropriate for CP Med.

Clients often ask why mediation may not move forward. Do not tell them! If they are made aware of what the mediator is looking for, they may modify their answers based on their desire to participate in mediation or to not participate. A way around that is to tell clients that mediation will move forward if the mediator feels they can be of assistance to the family, and keep everyone safe physically and emotionally.

Although the decision to screen a case out of mediation may happen early in the process, it is important not to officially make the determination until all of the parties, including CAS, have been met. Waiting helps to avoid perceived blame. Also, there is to be no reason given to the parties as to why mediation has not moved forward. A good way to explain this to people is to tell them that if the group is given a reason, it lays blame, and that is not helpful. Also, all of the information gathered by the mediator up until that point is confidential, and cannot be shared. It saves a lot of stress for the mediator and confusion for the parties if this is clarified early in the intake process.

Appendix D shows a standard form that I use during an intake appointment with a family member. There are certain common questions that I ask, so I created a template to remind me to gather that information.

INDIAN OR NATIVE

It is important to know if the child is Indian or Native, as they are entitled to Aboriginal Dispute Resolution processes if the family wishes.

This question also highlights cultural sensitivity. Terminology is always changing. The terms "Indian" & "Native" are used throughout this book, as they are the terms in the legislation. When meeting with someone of a different cultural background than yourself, ask them for their preferred terminology. For example, some people prefer the terms "Indigenous" or "First Nations." Also, give the participants permission to correct you with respect to terminology if it is something they find offensive. That demonstrates an openness to learn, and people generally respect that.

INDEPENDENT LEGAL ADVICE

It is also important to know if the client has a lawyer, or has received Independent Legal Advice (ILA). If the client has not received ILA, the mediator has a responsibility to encourage the client to seek ILA. They are a parent, and they are involved with CAS. They have certain rights and responsibilities, and a lawyer is the best person to inform the clients of these items. If the client has retained a lawyer, there may be an expense for any conversation between the lawyer and the mediator. As a result, the mediator should ask the client if they want the mediator to contact the lawyer.

COURT:

Knowing whether or not the matter is before the court can provide helpful information as to potential timelines, and level of cooperation between the parties. It is also helpful to know if the matter is in Family Court or CAS Court. If the matter is in CAS Court, there may be a sense of greater conflict between the family and CAS, or CAS has used a more intrusive intervention (i.e. apprehension).

This is also a good opportunity to explain to family members about the possibility of a lawyer being appointed for the child. There are times when workers may not have informed family members of this. In those cases, it can be quite stressful for a person to receive a call from a lawyer, and not know the context. By informing them ahead of time, it helps to reduce surprises and potential anxiety.

CONTACT RESTRICTIONS:

Restrictions refers to Restraining Orders, Peace Bonds, Bail Conditions etc. It is incredibly important to know if there are any legal restrictions in place preventing any of the parties from having contact with one another. If there are conditions that the parties not communicate, there is a possibility that one or both of the parties may be charged if they continue in mediation. It is the responsibility of the parties to have the conditions varied by whomever imposed the conditions. Keep in mind that shuttle mediation still counts as "indirect contact," and could result in charges if certain restrictions are not in place.

It is also important to understand that the parties cannot simply inform the mediator that they consent to varying the conditions. Without legal documentation confirming that the conditions have been varied, the mediator must operate as if the conditions remain in place and are enforceable. Best practice is to request a copy of the conditions and any variance for the file.

INTERVIEW CHILDREN:

In recent years, there has been a shift to include the child's voice in the mediation process. This will be covered later in the chapter "Voice of the Child." If the mediator is a proponent of a child-inclusive mediation process, is should be discussed with the parents/ caregivers of the child. Unless the child is a Crown Ward, the mediator must have the permission of the parents/ caregivers to interview the child. If either of the parents does not consent, the mediator needs to have some discussion with the parents to understand their reasoning. This may have an impact as to whether or not the mediation moves forward.

Be sure to enquire about the ages of the children, and their overall well-being. The process is focussed on the best interests and safety of the children. The mediator should have some sense of how the children are doing, any behaviour or mental health challenges, and especially if the current situation is having an impact on them. Although the responses are often skewed to reflect the parent's position, the mediator will gain insight into the well-being of the children, and the relationship between the children and the parties.

HISTORY:

When meeting the family members, the mediator needs to understand the family's perspective as to why CAS is involved, and the dynamics between the different family members. The mediator needs to ensure each participant's intake appointment is treated as a blank canvas before starting. It is also critical that the mediator not share information from anyone else's intake appointment; including that of the worker's intake appointment.

It is very common to have an image in your mind of the case dynamics based on one intake, only to have them completely changed by the end of the intake with another person. Leaving assumptions out of the meeting is critical to ensure the mediator understands the client's situation from the client's perspective. Perception is equal to reality, and how the client perceives the situation will have a tremendous impact on the mediation process.

SCREENING FOR FAMILY VIOLENCE, ABUSE & POWER IMBALANCES:

There are many different screening tools in place, and different mediators have their preferences. Screening is an ongoing process in mediation, and it begins as soon as the file is received. The mediator needs to explore any history of power and control, verbal and/ or emotional abuse, physical violence, mental health, and substance use. It is also important to explore whether or not the parties will be able to manage in the same room. If clients are uncomfortable with the idea of being in the same room, explore the reasons and with that information, a decision can be made as to whether or not a shuttle mediation is more fitting.

STRENGTHS:

Many of the cases seen today in CP Med are custody and access cases. These files often have long-standing conflict, and the parties have become very entrenched in their opinions. If they are involved in litigation, there has also no doubt been documentation filed highlighting as many negative opinions as possible about each other. Asking about strengths of the other parties is a way to help parents shift their thinking. If the parent struggles to find a strength, ask them for a strength from the child's perspective.

MENTAL HEALTH:

As a result of TV and social media, the conversation of mental health is much more prevalent these days, but pop psychology is not new. Unfortunately, this also leads to a plethora of informal diagnoses. The most common ones I hear are Bi-Polar Disorder, Personality Disorder, and Post Traumatic Stress Disorder. Many people either diagnose themselves or the people around them without any real training or education on the matter.

That said, it is important to get a sense of everyone's mental health and any formal diagnoses. Be sure to ask the participants if there are any mental health concerns for themselves or the other party. If they offer a "diagnosis," follow up to discuss the symptomatology. It is not the mediator's role to diagnosis mental health, but having an understanding of client behaviours and attitudes will help the mediator to better manage the joint mediation session. The mediator also needs to enquire about any past or current treatment for the mental health concerns.

If an individual appears to be mentally and/ or emotionally unstable, mediation should not proceed at this time.

SUBSTANCE USE:

In our culture, substance use is becoming more common, and more acceptable. In the past, alcohol was the only acceptable substance to ingest but with changing laws around marijuana, that is also becoming more common. There also appears to be a growing opiate problem in different parts of the country. Regardless of the substance, the mediator should ask all of the participants if there are any concerns with respect to substance use for themselves or for the other party. If so, has there ever been or is there currently any treatment?

When dealing with substance use, the mediator should focus on the effect of the substance use on the child, and less on the actual substance itself. If the substance use is having a negative impact on the child, there is reason for concern. The mediator must be aware of the difference between recreational use and problem use, and hold their personal prejudices in check. They must also filter the information received to determine if the use is actually having a negative impact, or if the client is providing their own personal bias about substance use.

If either of the parties is actively using substances, and the substance is having a negative impact on the family dynamic, the mediator needs to have further discussions with the participants. Substance use can impact a person's ability to make good decisions, and affect them even when they are not under the influence. Under no circumstances should an intake or joint mediation session proceed if anyone appears to be impaired.

ADDICTION:

Addiction is another area for discussion. Although many people focus on substance use, there are many addictions from which a person can suffer. Addiction can be defined as a physiological and psychological dependence that is beyond voluntary control. It is an obsessive compulsion to which a person becomes powerless both physically and mentally. Even addictions that are not typically seen as physical (eg gambling, shopping etc), have a biological component as there is a neurochemical (dopamine) release in the brain during the activity. Dopamine is a neurotransmitter that helps control the brain's reward and pleasure centres.

Moreover, it is also important to understand that many addictions stem from a trauma background. Oftentimes, substance use is due to self-medicating traumatic symptoms. Pain may also be a factor in developing an addiction, as many opiate addictions begin from a doctor's prescription. The stigma and shame associated with addictions are a large reason why a person will try to hide their addiction.

It's important to explore if there are any concerns with respect to addictions and if so, to what extent they impact the children and the parenting relationship. Examples of addiction include but are not limited to:

- drugs (prescription, non-prescription, inhalants)
- alcohol
- gambling (online, casino's etc)
- sex (pornography, massage parlours/ prostitutes, masturbation etc)
- food (emotional eating, binging and purging etc)
- video games
- working
- exercise
- shopping

In the event that any of the parties discloses a past or present addiction, the mediator should explore if any treatment has been sought. If treatment occurred, there should be discussion about the type of treatment but more importantly, the effectiveness of the treatment.

Relapse is often a part of the recovery process, but attention should be placed on the long-term outcomes There are many types of substance abuse programs that offer medical treatments (eg methadone or soboxone for opiate addiction) but more often than not, a successful treatment program includes a psychological component to understand the reasons for use (eg trauma, coping strategies etc), how best to deal with triggers, and to create an identity where sobriety exists. It is worth noting that for some people, sobriety and abstinence are not one in the same. Sobriety can mean different things for different people and different addictions.

The mediator should explore this topic with the parties as even those in the same family dealing with the same issue may have a different definition or desired outcome. Understanding this information will help the mediator manage the situation if the addiction issue is raised during the joint mediation session.

SUPPORT PERSON:

Often during the intake process, people will ask to bring a support person to the joint mediation session. Whether or not a participant brings a support person is their choice. None of the other participants have the ability to deny a support person. They do however, have the ability to say they will not sit in the same room as the support person. They may also choose not to participate if a certain support person is present.

If a participant indicates that they would like to bring a support person, the mediator should discuss this with the client. It is important to process why the participant feels it is necessary to bring a support person, and there should also be discussion as to how they think the other parties will react. The mediator needs to ensure that all participants know that if they wish to bring a support person to the joint mediation session, they need to inform the mediator of this beforehand.

The mediator has an obligation to inform the other parties that someone is bringing a support person, and who the support person will be. The mediator should then also ask the other parties if they would like to bring a support person. It can be problematic if someone arrives at the joint mediation session with a support person, and nobody knew about it ahead of time.

SURPRISES = DRAMA

As mentioned, the choice of support person is that of the individual participant. It may be a family member, a friend, or even their lawyer. The role of the support person is very specific, and should be reviewed with the participant and support person before the joint mediation session. Regardless of the support person's connection with the participant, they are attending the mediation as support. They are not the one engaged in the negotiation. This requires special attention when lawyers are present, as the lawyer's role is to be a client's advocate. In the joint mediation session however, their role is to provide advice, and offer suggestions. The mediator should define these boundaries clearly before the joint mediation session begins. Failure to do so may create further challenges in the mediation.

SCHEDULING:

Prior to ending the intake appointment, it is useful to ask clients if there are preferred days or times to meet for a joint mediation session if the mediation moves forward. This will save time when scheduling the joint session. If the mediator has a sense of the clients' availability, they can start from there when looking at their own calendars. This will avoid multiple emails, phone calls etc to schedule appointments. If the determination is to do a shuttle mediation, ensure that clients are scheduled for different arrival times.

WORKER

The worker's intake appointment is very similar to the family member's intake appointment. In the spirit of maintaining neutrality and treating everyone as equals, the worker also signs the confidentiality agreement. This also makes worker's aware of the experience that family members go through during the intake process. Although I do not read the Confidentiality Agreement to workers, some time is still spent on explaining what each paragraph means. It is also important during their intake to remind the worker that they are not permitted to take any notes on the day of the joint mediation session. An example of a Worker Intake Form can be seen in *Appendix E*.

OCL:

The mediator should ask the worker if OCL has been notified of the mediation referral. It is not uncommon for workers to respond with "It's not in court." Remind the workers that the OCL needs to be informed of every case that is referred to mediation, using the prescribed Notice of ADR form. If the referral has been submitted, the mediator should enquire as to whether or not the OCL has made a decision with respect to their involvement. It is acceptable for the mediator to reach out to the OCL directly.

If a lawyer is already involved to represent the child, the mediator needs to ensure that the worker has informed the lawyer of the mediation referral.

CONTACT RESTRICTIONS:

In the event that there are contact restrictions in place, workers often have a copy of the conditions in their file. If possible, review the conditions with the worker, and discuss whether or not a variance is required. If so, ask the worker to reach out to the family, so that the family may begin the process of getting a variance. It is also helpful if the worker writes a letter to the necessary person (e.g. Probation Officer, Crown Attorney etc), supporting a variance for the purposes of CP Med.

INTERVIEW CHILDREN:

Spend some time with the worker discussing how the children are doing, and how they are impacted by the situation requiring CAS intervention. The worker will have valuable insight into the well-being of the children, and also have suggestions on how to engage the child in an interview. Workers are often actively engaged with service providers connected with the children, and are often able to help determine if there is a benefit to meeting with the children as part of the mediation process.

HISTORY:

When meeting with the worker, the mediator needs to ask questions as to when the CAS file opened, reason for service, and any changes since the file opened. The mediator must also explore any incidents of domestic violence (physical, emotional and/ or verbal), intimidation, and/ or control. CAS will also often have information related to a participants' substance use and mental health. The mediator should also ask if the worker has any concerns with the idea of the parties being in the room together, or with being in the same room themselves with the family members.

SUPPORT PERSON:

The mediator should spend some time with the worker to explain the support person concept. As with family members, workers may also have feelings about a family member's choice in support person. The choice however, is the individual participant's. In general, CAS supervisors and/ or CAS lawyers do not attend the group mediation session unless the family members are bringing their lawyers. There is a perceived power imbalance towards CAS by virtue of their authority, and having multiple CAS staff present during a joint mediation session may be very intimidating to family members.

SCHEDULING:

Explore scheduling with the worker. Most CAS agencies have standard hours of operation from 8:30am to 4:30pm or 9am to 5pm Monday to Friday. Although there is always After-Hours coverage, the majority of CAS staff work during the day. Although many of our families are not working, there are many that are working; some of them "working poor." If they take time off work, some run the risk of losing their job. The mediator needs to have discussions with the worker as to whether or not the worker is available for evening appointments and/ or weekend appointments. The mediator should also be open to this concept if they are going to adequately service the child welfare population.

Bottom Lines:

The mediator should strongly recommend that the worker have a case consultation/ supervision with their supervisor prior to the mediation. During that supervision, the worker and supervisor should brainstorm potential outcomes that may be suggested by the family members during the mediation. That way, the worker will be in a better position to make decisions during the mediation without the need for additional consultation with their supervisor.

The mediator should also encourage the worker to have conversations with the family members prior to the group mediation session. The worker should explain to families if there are certain issues that are not open for discussion. An example of this may be placement of the children. The CAS may have a position that a child will not be returned to a parent's care, and the mediation is to discuss access. The parent needs to be aware of this ahead of time, so they are not disappointed if they feel the mediation is to discuss reintegration.

If possible and the family members are comfortable with the idea, they too should inform the other parties if there are topics not open for discussion. Although it may narrow the mediation subject matter, it may also prevent an unnecessary waste of everyone's time.

SAFE TERMINATION

Not all mediations go forward, and there are many reasons why this is the case. Ultimately, it is up to the mediator's discretion if they believe that they can facilitate a process that is beneficial and safe. If not, they have an obligation to screen the case out. Informing the clients that mediation is not moving forward may be done differently by different mediators, but there is an obligation to do so in a safe way. Remember, although the final decision to screen out comes later, safe termination begins during the intake introductions.

When a decision is made to terminate the mediation, best practice is to phone the parties to inform them. It is also beneficial to send a Closing Letter to all of the parties indicating that the mediation is not moving forward. In the Closing Letter, indicate that the mediation is not moving forward, and that the reasons cannot be disclosed. A suggestion is to also include a statement that says the decision is not a reflection on any one person.

If the case has been screened out and there is a more suitable process than mediation, it is ok to inform the parties of the other process. Be certain to provide all of the parties with the same information, so that there are no misunderstandings. Depending on the reasons and the mediator's comfort level, it may also be possible to indicate why the other process may be more suitable. Use discretion however, as this may put people at risk. What the mediator says during these conversations is not always what the clients hear.

Some clients are happy that their file has been screened out of mediation, and others are disappointed. The mediator may receive inquiries as to why the mediation is not moving forward and sometimes, clients will become very persistent in their requests for mediation to move ahead. The mediator must remain careful about the information they provide. Once they have made a decision to terminate the mediation, barring any new information, the mediation should be terminated. When in doubt, the mediator needs to follow their gut instincts about the people and the case.

VOICE OF THE CHILD

The United Nations Convention on the Rights of a Child and the CFSA define a child as any person under the age of eighteen (18). In Section 37 (1) of the CFSA however, a child is further defined as a person under the age of sixteen (16) unless there is already a court finding of a child in need of protection. That is to say that unless there is an existing finding, CAS is not able to provide protection services to children aged sixteen (16) to eighteen (18). Furthermore, children aged sixteen (16) to eighteen (18), are entitled to refuse services offered by CAS. It has been tabled that the age of protection service eligibility increase to eighteen (18), however this has not been approved as of yet.

As mentioned earlier, there has been a shift in mediation in recent years to include the voice of the child. There are some who feel meeting with the child only serves to bring them further into the conflict. Truth be told however, the children are often already very much involved in the situation as a direct result of the adults. When looking at the best interests of a child, it is helpful to have an understanding of the child's views and experiences.

NOTHING ABOUT ME WITHOUT ME

Prior to making a determination as to whether or not to meet with a child, the mediator needs to have completed intakes with all of the adult parties, and determined that the case is suitable for mediation. The mediator must assess whether there is benefit to meeting with the child or if it will do more harm. Many children involved in the child welfare system have been interviewed many times by many different people.

The mediator needs to be sensitive to that fact, and not over-interview the child.

The mediator should not meet with children unless they have completed training on how to appropriately interview children. Interviewing a seven (7) year old is very different than interviewing a fifteen (15) year old, and the mediator must know how to interact with the child in an age-appropriate manner. The mediator's goal of meeting with the child is to get a sense of who is in the child's life, and how they are managing with the current situation. It is imperative that the mediator not conduct a "Safety Interview" in the same manner as a CAS worker. Occasionally however, a disclosure does happen. If this occurs, the mediator needs to know how to manage that situation, and do the least possible harm to the child and to any possible investigation after the fact.

The mediator should only meet with the children if there is a perceived benefit to meeting with them. Meeting with children just for the sake of meeting with them serves no purpose other than financial gain for the mediator. If the mediator feels they are missing valuable information or the parents' understanding of the child's wishes are grossly different, there is merit to meeting with the child. It is also helpful at the joint mediation session if the mediator is able to reference the child with first-hand knowledge, and describe certain personality traits of the child. This helps clients to focus on why they are in mediation; for the best interests of the child.

If a lawyer is appointed by the OCL to represent the child in the CP Med process, the child's lawyer then becomes the mediator's gatekeeper to the child. The lawyer will decide if the mediator meets with the child.

The lawyer will also decide in consultation with their client, in what capacity the child will participate in the mediation. If the

child is young, it is unlikely that they will attend the joint mediation session. If the child is older however, they may attend. Some ways in which children can participate in the joint mediation sessions include but are not limited to:
- child not physically present but their lawyer attends
- in the same room (with lawyer present)
- in a different room (with their lawyer)
- in a different room (lawyer with the adults and providing child with updates)

The lawyer and mediator together will determine the best method of sharing the child's views and preferences with the adults. Ways in which the child's lawyer may share the child's views and preferences include but are not limited to:
- to the group at the beginning of the joint mediation session
- to the group throughout the joint mediation session
- to each adult privately with the mediator present
- to each parent privately with the child and mediator present

If an OCL is appointed and/ or the Eligibility Spectrum Code is a 4-2 (Parent-Child Conflict), the child is an equal party to the mediation; much the same way the child would be an equal in the eyes of the court if an OCL was appointed. That means that they have just as much ability to say 'Yes' or 'No' to anything in the mediation, and their agreement is necessary for an item to be included in the Memorandum of Understanding. That said, OCL lawyers often encourage the parents to take ownership of child-related decisions in an effort to take pressure off of the children. For example, parents may reach an agreement with respect to the child's schedule and the child may not be in complete agreement. Barring any significant worries, the lawyer will is likely to support the parents' agreement as it is in the best interests of their client.

As with the adults, the child's interview is confidential. The mediator needs to explain this to the child at the beginning of the meeting. Although the mediator meets with the child privately (unless OCL is assigned and present), it is helpful to have the conversation of confidentiality with the parent present. It takes the pressure off the child if an adult asks later what they spoke about, and the child does not want to share. At the end of the child's interview, the mediator should ask the child's permission to share specific content that may be useful in the joint mediation session. If the child does not consent, the information remains confidential.

JOINT MEDIATION SESSION(S)

Ideally, joint mediation sessions are scheduled at a neutral location, and away from the courthouse, CAS offices, or at the office of one of the lawyers. Exceptions to this can be made on consent of the parties, but the mediator must take special care to ensure the parties are agreeing of their own will, and not due to pressure from others. That includes pressure from the mediator to hold the joint mediation session at their location of preference. As discussed in the Intake chapter, many mediators services many geographical locations, and it has become more acceptable to hold joint mediation sessions at the CAS office. There may be other reasons for using a location such as the CAS office as well, including but not limited to, a need for security.

In CP Med, an agent from CAS must be present for the joint mediation session(s). CAS has an interest in the outcome, and is considered one of the parties. Furthermore, CAS will be responsible for monitoring how the agreement is carried out, as well as assisting with the implementation of the agreement. If the CAS does not have an interest in the outcome and are not present for the joint mediation session, it is no longer a CP Med. It becomes a Family Mediation. Family Mediation is not funded by MCYS.

If a lawyer has been appointed to represent the child in the mediation process, the lawyer must also be present for the joint mediation sessions. This is especially important if the matter is before the court, and the parties intend on making the agreement into a court order.

The mediator needs to be early for the joint mediation session to make sure that the rooms are ready to accommodate the parties upon their arrival. This will prevent any of the parties from spending an excessive amount of time in the waiting area. If the mediator is planning to hold a shuttle mediation, the parties should be given varying arrival times to avoid any client contact in the parking lot, waiting room etc.

Once the parties are in the room for the joint mediation session, the mediator will establish some housekeeping items. If there have been any no-contact conditions among the parties, the joint mediation session should only be occurring if there has been a variance of some sort. The mediator should let the parties know of this variance at the outset, as one or more of the parties may be very nervous about that issue.

Remind the parties that all communication up until that point in time is confidential, and cannot be shared. The mediator is essentially starting with a clean slate. Inform the parties that once the Agreement To Mediate (ATM) is signed, all communication is for the group; even if the parties are in separate rooms. If the parties wish to have a confidential conversation (caucus) with the mediator after the ATM is signed, the party must inform the mediator that the content is confidential.

It is also a good time to remind clients that the focus is on the future. What has happened up until that point in time is done, and in the past. It cannot be changed. Although the mediator may need to discuss the past somewhat, the past cannot dominate the session. The focus needs to be shifting to the future, and in doing things differently.

FOCUS ON FORWARD

Spend some time explaining that the joint mediation sessions are without prejudice settlement discussions. That is to say that the content of the meetings will not be used against anyone, people have the ability to change their minds, and the ultimate goal is to make progress towards an agreement. This is a good opportunity to remind all of the parties that the mediator is the only person who may take notes. Workers may enter a casenote indicating that they attended mediation on that date and who was present but in reality, they do not even need to document that. The only documentation that comes out of the joint mediation session is the Memorandum of Understanding (MOU).

AGREEMENT TO MEDIATE

Policy Directive CW 005-06 is very clear that an Agreement to Mediate (ATM) *should* be used in the CP Med process. The ATM specifically needs to outline the confidentiality provisions of the CP Med process contained in the Regulation. These provisions need to be clearly explained to all of the parties at the beginning of the joint mediation session or earlier, so that the parties are able to make informed decisions about their participation.

The Policy Directive further notes that having a written ATM may act as a disincentive for some people. This would likely apply to individuals with literacy issues. If the parties do not sign a written ATM, the mediator must ensure that the confidentiality provisions are reviewed with the parties, understood, and agreed to by the parties. In the event that a written ATM is not signed by the participants, the Policy Directive states that the worker MUST document the reasons in the family's file.

In an effort to streamline the process and avoid miscommunication, it is beneficial to read the ATM to all of the parties at the beginning of the joint mediation. It will save time as everyone hears the content at once instead of waiting for each participant to read the document. Also, it can avoid having people feeling marginalized if they have literacy challenges. It is helpful to circulate a copy of the ATM, so participants can follow along while the mediator is reading the ATM. Best practice is that the mediator explain each part of the ATM clearly to all of the parties, and also offer the parties a copy of the signed ATM. That way, participants may further review the document at a later date.

An example of a standard ATM can be found in *Appendix F*.

Background Information

After the parties sign the ATM, the mediator needs to acquire some background information. This is valuable information to include at the beginning of the MOU. It may also help to begin some of the conversations in the joint mediation session. Some background information to collect includes, but is not limited to:

- the children's names and dates of birth
- if children are Indian or Native and if so, what band
- if the matter is before the court and if so, which court (Family Court or CAS court), and when it returns to court
- if the parties have retained lawyers and if so, the names of their lawyers
- Date of Marriage (if applicable) and Date of Separation (if applicable)
- when the CAS file opened

First and foremost, the mediator needs to have the correct spelling of the names of the children, and their dates of birth. The mediator should also differentiate if there are other children connected to the file, but not a subject of the mediation. That is, clients may have children with other partners with whom they are not in mediation.

If the parties have not retained a lawyer, the mediator should list whether or not the parties have sought out Independent Legal Advice. For any judge and/ or lawyer reviewing the MOU at a later date, it will prompt them to ask questions as to whether or not the party fully understands the MOU. It also highlights that the mediator asked the parties if they had received Independent Legal Advice and if they had not, the mediator likely encouraged them to seek out Independent Legal Advice.

If the mediation referral is with respect to adult conflict or custody and access, knowing the date of marriage and date of separation may help the mediator to explore how long the conflict has been going on. It may also provide some options to explore times when the family was not engaged in the same level of conflict.

Much like date of separation, having a rough idea of when the CAS file opened and reason for service may also provide insight as to how long the family has been struggling with the issue at hand. It also provides an opportunity to explore any changes that have occurred during that time and specifically, any progress the family has made.

SHUTTLE MEDIATION

Shuttle mediation is when the parties are in separate rooms, and the mediator travels back-and-forth. Reasons for using shuttle mediation include but are not limited to:

- one person's fear of another party
- possible physical intimidation
- physical and/ or emotional safety
- high level of conflict → it may be beneficial for the mediator to share the information in an effort to take the emotionality out of the content
- issues involving a support person → seeing them may create increased emotionality/ conflict

When using shuttle mediation, the mediator needs to review some guidelines with the parties at the beginning of the joint mediation session. Some guidelines include but are not limited to:

- no party will try to enter the room of any of the other parties unless approved by the mediator, and with the mediator present
- leaving the room (eg smoke breaks, bathroom breaks etc) should be strategized with the mediator in an effort to avoid the parties from being in contact with each other. This is particularly important if the mediator thinks either of the parties may leave the building at any time.
- reminding parties that there may be extended periods of time when the mediator is not in the room, and with the other party. Time with each party may not always be equal, and will vary based on the issues being discussed.

If the mediation involves parents on opposing sides, the worker generally travels back-and-forth with the mediator. Often during a custody and access CP Med, the bulk of the negotiation is done between the parents. The worker is there to provide suggestions and intercept any unsuitable plans in their estimation and as a result, they need to be privy to the dialogue. The parties can however, still have conversations with the mediator without the worker present. When reviewing the ATM, remind parties that during a shuttle mediation, content disclosed in one room is shareable in the other room, unless the party asks that it not be shared.

If facilitating a shuttle mediation, the ATM to is reviewed in each room. The background information is also reviewed in each room. When one of the parties provides background information to the mediator, clarify its accuracy with the other party. If there are any discrepancies, the mediator needs to discuss this with the parties. If the parties cannot agree on the specifics of any background information, it should not be included in the MOU.

SAFE TERMINATION

At the end of a successful mediation, the mediator will review the points of agreement with the parties. This ensures that there are no surprises when the parties receive the MOU. The mediator can provide any necessary clarification, and give the parties an idea of how the MOU will be written.

The end of the mediation session is another opportunity to remind the parties of their equality in the mediation process. Ask the parties how they would like to receive the MOU, and inform them that it will be sent to all of the parties via the same delivery method. That way, there is no perception of favouritism amongst the parties. If any of the parties requests that the MOU be sent via traditional mail, the MOU should be sent to all parties via traditional mail. This is because traditional mail is generally a slower mode of delivery.

Nowadays, the most common method of delivery is via email. When sending the MOU via email, ensure the parties are told at the joint mediation session that you will not make substantive changes to the MOU via email. The mediator may make corrections to details (ie wrong date, spelling error etc), but changes to the actual content of the agreement should not be amended outside of the actual mediation sessions. Changing the MOU based on an email from only one (1) person can fuel conflict unnecessarily.

Another important point when sending emails to parties is to discuss whether or not their individual email addresses may be displayed. When emailing multiple parties at the same time during the intake phase, it is best to ensure that addresses are blind copied. At the joint mediation session, ask for consent to display email addresses. If all of the parties consent to their address being displayed, the mediator may display the addresses. Then, the parties may "Reply To All" if there is a correction to be made on the MOU, and everyone is aware of the dialogue.

If there is going to be another joint mediation session, this is the ideal time to schedule the appointment. With technology today, most people have their cell phone with them, and their calendar is on their phone. Discussing upcoming appointments is easiest in real-time, and not via emails and phone calls after the fact.

Depending on the dynamics between the parties, it may be useful to have them leave at separate times. This is especially true in a shuttle mediation. In a shuttle mediation, the mediator should first wrap up with the at-risk person/ person who requested shuttle mediation. That will give the party an opportunity to leave the area while the mediator is finishing up with the other person.

Not all mediations end on a positive note. There are times when one of the parties will end the process, and times when the mediator ends the process. Oftentimes when a client ends the process, they will leave the room and/ or building ahead of everyone. More often than not, the party is angry or frustrated. When this happens, it is important to debrief with the remaining parties to discuss safety when leaving. If there are concerns for safety, the other parties should be escorted to their vehicles, or have someone pick them up. In some instances it may be necessary to contact police to ask for assistance.

If the mediator ends the mediation, the mediator should debrief with each of the parties. The mediator should be careful as to what information they provide the parties, and be careful not to place blame on anyone. It is acceptable for the mediator to explain that mediation is ending, because the mediator does not believe the parties will come to an agreement.

MEMORANDUM OF UNDERSTANDING

The Memorandum of Understanding (MOU) is the document that the mediator sends to the parties following the mediation. It is a list of agreements reached in principle. In a CP Med, it does not list any of the items of which the parties did not agree. The MOU is not legally binding when the mediator sends it, and the mediator should NOT be having clients sign the MOU in their presence.

At the end of the joint mediation session(s), parties are once again directed to get legal advice. They should have a lawyer review the MOU, and give their opinion on its contents. A lawyer will ensure that the participant fully understands the document, and its implications. The lawyer will also offer suggestions on any items that need further discussion or changes.

The MOU is a flexible document. Parties have the ability to change their mind on any of its contents. The mediator should however, encourage the parties to inform one another if they intend on making changes. If the parties make changes to how they will act out the MOU without informing the other parties, it will lead to further conflict.

Although, the MOU is not legally binding, it does become an expectation of CAS. If parties make changes in the implementation of the MOU without informing CAS, they should be prepared for CAS to follow up and ask questions.

Different mediators have different approaches to the structure of the MOU. Some believe that it should be written in plain language. They believe that terms with legal connotations such as "shall" should be replaced with "will." Although these words have the same meaning, some mediators feel using the word "shall" makes the MOU sound too much like a legal document.

There are other mediators however, who prefer to use legal terminology and language. Their feeling is that it will be more cost effective for the clients after the fact to have the MOU made into a legally-binding document. Regardless of your approach, the most important thing to remember is that the MOU needs to be written in a way that clients, including family members understand.

When sending the MOU via email, it is best to send the file in pdf format. Some mediators will also encrypt the document as an added safety measure. Sending the MOU in pdf format makes it more difficult for the parties to edit the document. Ultimately, the MOU is the clients' document, and it is "in principle." So, any of the clients may change of the points of the MOU to whatever suits them best. For the mediator however, they should makes attempts to protect the content so anything with their name on it is actually their words.

The MOU should only be sent to a party's lawyer with the consent of the party.

WHAT *NOT* TO DO

Book Joint Mediation Sessions Before All Intakes Completed

Booking joint mediation sessions before completing all of the intakes can give parties false hope. If the mediation then does not move forward, it can set up further conflict among the parties. An exception to this may be if there is a pending court date, and it is made VERY clear to ALL of the parties that there is still a chance that the mediation may not move forward based on the intakes of all parties. Further, a decision would not be provided until all of the parties have been met.

Disclose Content From An Intake Appointment

Information in a person's intake appointment is confidential; including the intake of CAS. It is not the mediator's role to explain to family members why CAS is involved or why CAS thinks mediation may be helpful. Sharing information from a family member's intake to another person's intake may put people at risk of harm, or derail the mediation process. Some parties may become angry if they learn that another party disclosed violence, control, or fear.

Disclose Dates/ Times Of Intake Appointments

It is virtually impossible for a mediator to have every last bit of information. No matter how good a job the mediator does at screening, there always remains a risk that something is missed. As a result, dates and times of intake appointments (or arrival times in a shuttle mediation) should not be shared, because the mediator has no way of knowing exactly what actions another party may take.

Disclose Why Mediation Was Screened Out

Disclosing why a mediation file is screened out often feels like blame to one of the parties. If certain parties feel blamed for mediation not moving ahead, it may put others at risk or harm. Exceptions to this is if the mediator recommends another process. Then, the mediator may tell the parties of the suggested alternate method(s).

Facilitate Joint Mediation Session(s) Without CAS Present

An agent from CAS MUST be present for the joint mediation session. They are considered a party to the mediation. If CAS is not present, it is NOT a CP Med. As a result, MCYS should not be paying for the mediation.

Display Email Addresses Without Consent

Some clients do not want any of their personal information shared with the other parties. Doing so is a breach of their trust, and may put people at risk of harm. It is also best practice to ask about consent to display email addresses in a private conversation; not during a meeting with multiple parties.

Sign Memorandum Of Understanding

There is specific criteria required for a document to meet the threshold of a domestic contract. Signing a mediated agreement MAY meet that threshold, and create a legally binding document. The MOU should not be signed by the parties with the mediator, as there is an expectation that the parties will seek out Independent Legal Advice after the mediation. If the parties chose to sign the MOU, that is their prerogative. However, under no circumstances should the mediator sign the MOU as a witness.

Send MOU To Worker To Proof-Read And Approve

CAS is a party, just like all of the other parties to the mediation. Sending the MOU to them for approval or to proof-read demonstrates a lack of neutrality. If the mediator is not confident in their MOU-writing ability or would like their documentation proof-read, they should send it to a peer to review; not to a mediation party.

CONCLUSION

The information contained herein is not comprehensive. It is not everything. It is a starting point, and an additional resource. Anyone considering CP Med should ensure that they have read the most recent version of the CFSA, the most up-to-date version of Ontario Regular 496/ 06 and the most up-to-date version of Policy Directive CW 005-06 in their entirety, and understand the contents of each.

FUNCTIONAL DEFINITIONS OF MEDIATION

'A' Not 'B'
'B' Not 'A'
Both 'A' and 'B'
Neither 'A' Nor 'B'

No two cases are exactly the same and what works in one situation, may not work in another. Sometimes "technique" A will work, but not B. Other times B will work, but not A. There are occasions when both A and B will work, and others where neither will work.

This emphasizes the mediator's need to stay current on research, and changing practices. We will never know it all but being open to new ideas, and an ability to think quickly, will help clients to resolve the issues at hand.

Assess
Adapt
Improvise

Identify
Assess
Manage

Never Say Never
Never Say Always

ARTICLES

STICKS & STONES
(October 5, 2012)

*"Sticks and Stones May Break My Bones
But Names Will Never Hurt Me"*

I think it's safe to say that just about every one of us has heard the above statement before. I also think that it's safe to say that the first time we heard it was probably from one of our parents. This phrase is typically expressed when a child complains of being called names in the school yard, or being picked on for being different. While our parents meant well by using this phrase, did they really understand what they were saying?

The truth of the matter is that the title phrase is elementary. While it outlines the risks of physical injury, it does not acknowledge the complexity of emotional wounds. It also implies that physical injury is more concerning than emotional injury.

In general, most physical injuries can be seen; especially when we're talking about the effects of being in contact with sticks and stones. Furthermore, physical injuries sustained from such an event are generally easily treatable. Emotional injuries however, are quite different. They may include depression, aggression, sadness, or even lack of any reaction. Let's take a closer look.

Yes, it is true that sticks and stones may break my bones. As a child, I fell and broke my wrist. While at car accidents as a firefighter, I have seen many people with cuts and broken bones. During my work in child welfare, I was involved in a case where a three year old child was severely burned on his forearm by his caregiver. It was never made clear if the burn was intentional, but he also had several bruises on his body in various locations. All of these examples clearly detail physical injury.

With all of the examples listed above, the physical treatment is straight-forward. For the broken bones, have them reset and put a cast on the limb. The cuts may require stitches. After a week, the stitches are removed and the patient may keep a visible scar. For the burned child, he was removed from the caregiver's home, and the burn treated. He was left with a scar on the posterior of his forearm and hand. In each case, the individual was able to carry on a normal life after the physical injury healed.

Now, let's look at "Names will never hurt me." Bullying, failed relationships, uncertainty of sexuality, abuse (verbal, physical, emotional, sexual), and lack of emotional support may all lead to the same thing; emotional injury. There are many other examples, but these few help to highlight my point. Perhaps the greatest contributor to long-term emotional injury is lack of emotional support.

Each and every one of us has had situations in our life that have been upsetting. Some people carry the burden of that upset, while others find ways to let it go. If we do not develop ways to cope with emotional injury, we are left with emotional scars. Unlike the healed cut or broken bone, these scars are not easily visible to the naked eye, and require advanced technology to be seen at all in some chronic cases. We may see some outward signs of mental health difficulties such as violence, excessive crying, or mania, but there are many people with emotional wounds that we would never know about.

Think of how many people die by suicide, but their outward signs of depression were not noticed. They are often described as shy, introverted or different. Their withdrawn presentation may have been a sign but because it was not exceptionally different, it was not paid attention to. Then there are cases of murder by prominent members of the community followed by comments of "Such a nice boy." The deaths are an outward sign, but often noticed too late.

While every case of emotional injury does not lead to physical death, it may lead to some form of emotional death. Examples may include fear of commitment, being emotionally guarded, promiscuity, risk-taking, or addictions. Many people use some or all of the above to help mask the emotional wounds that they have and as a result, they miss out on possibly wonderful opportunities.

These incidents occur because of emotional injuries that have not been addressed by the person experiencing them. It's not accurate to say that the injuries are healed but rather, we learn to re-evaluate their meaningfulness in our lives. Left untreated, these injuries may begin to manifest themselves through behaviour issues, learning disabilities, suicide and more. In medicine, treatment implies a passive process. While some emotional injuries may be treated with medication, most often involve a much more active process. There are many avenues to explore but ultimately, the answer lies within the person who has been wounded.

As human beings, we must all do our best to help others develop the necessary tools of tolerance, compassion, and understanding. With this foundation, people will be more apt to seek assistance when they need it. They will also be more inclined to speak out against someone else being emotionally harmed. Whether a child or an adult, we all have a responsibility to help others, and to speak out against emotional harm. As family and friends, our role is not to tell people "I told you so" when they fall or feel down. Our role is to help them up, and tell them that we're there for them. That's the support they need.

FILLING THE VOID
(February 25, 2014)

For years, there has been discussion about *The Void* in martial arts. Much of what we study relates to filling the void during physical interaction. Once there has been physical contact between two people during a physical interaction, they become one physical entity. When contact is broken, a void is created between the previous points of contact. During much of my journey, I was under the impression that I needed to fill the void before my partner in order to dominate the situation. I was wrong!

I finally began to understand the concept of *Filling the Void* about one month ago; eleven months after my father died and over twenty-two years after I began martial arts training. The light bulb went off while in a counselling session when I was discussing the loss of my father. Yet another example of how the true study of martial arts is beyond the mats, and not just about physical drills.

During the conversation with my counsellor, I began to parallel physical interaction with relationships. When we care about someone, we create an emotional connection. This connection is similar to physical connection in the attacker-defender drills. When one of the people in the relationship is no longer present (break-up, death, personality change etc), a void is created. Once the void has been created, it needs to be filled. If it is not filled, the space remains empty. When thinking of the physical interaction, if the void is created and nobody moves to fill it, you're both stuck in place. The same happens in emotional relationships.

My father and I were incredibly close. I considered him my best friend, and we never struggled to find conversation. When he died, I was devastated. I had lost my best friend, my role model, my hero. This created a huge void in my life, and lots of intense, internal struggle.

My father died of cancer. He was diagnosed nine years before he died and really, he was pretty healthy for most of that time. As he got more ill, I found myself helping out more around my parents' home. When he finally died, I found myself taking on all of the maintenance responsibilities of their home, and also trying to be all things for my mother.

This created lots of internal conflict, because I was attempting to fill the void by being him. In some strange way, I was attempting to keep him alive by taking on his responsibilities. It was no longer a case of a child doing more for aging parents. It was me imposing myself as a surrogate. What made it even more difficult was that because I was so focussed on subconsciously keeping him alive, I was not working through my own grief.

Now, the void created by his death still needs to be filled. The question is with what intent. I've been filling the void, but in a very unhealthy manner. Now, I need to fill the void in a functional and healthy way. The way I'm doing this is by setting boundaries on my various roles in my personal life. Also when doing things my father normally would have done, I ask myself if I'm doing it to be him, to be like him, or to be the grown child of an aging parent. I also try to focus on positive memories, and lessons learned from my father. All of these things help me to fill the void in a healthier, more functional way.

Now, back to the mats and our martial arts scenario. Someone has thrown a strike at you, and you've redirected them. In your redirection, your hand had contact with their shoulder, but your hand came away from the shoulder. You have also taken your partner from a place of balance to a place of imbalance.

Several voids have been created, and those spaces need to be filled.

If you think that you must fill the void before your partner, you are more than likely filling the void in a destructive way. The goal is simply to be first which means you win, and they lose. If the partner moves first in an attempt to fill the void and you adjust to simply cause them harm/ imbalance, you've also entered into a destructive space.

The dilemma becomes intent. We must take into consideration why the void needs to be filled. What is the motivation? Is your partner filling the void to counter, or are they simply adjusting to retreat. If you harm someone who's trying to retreat, you've then become the negative in the interaction. Of course, it goes the other way too. Perhaps your motivation for filling the void is one of distance or retreat. If the idea is to neutralize and not destroy, the intent is positive.

When it comes to the voids in your life, you need to continually ask yourself what, why, and how. What is the void? Why am I trying to fill the void, and how am I going to fill the void in a healthy and functional way. Filling it blindly or ignoring it will create a state of imbalance both physically and emotionally.

THE FAMILY TRIANGLE
Using Geometry to Move Families Forward
January 24, 2017

Mediation is designed to assist people with working out differences, so that they are able to function better as parents while living separately. *The Family Triangle* is an effective tool in helping families shift their focus from the past to the present, and ultimately, to the future. While family relationships are complex, *The Family Triangle* provides a simplistic representation of the child-parent-parent relationship.

The concept of *The Family Triangle* is just that; a simple triangle. One (1) point represents the child, and one (1) point represents each parent. Further, the points are connected. In genealogy, the child would generally be seen at the bottom of the diagram. With *The Family Triangle*, the child is at the top. Visualizing the triangle in this way allows people to view the relationship from a structural perspective. There is a base (a foundation), a distinct top (a purpose), and everyone is connected.

Figure 1:

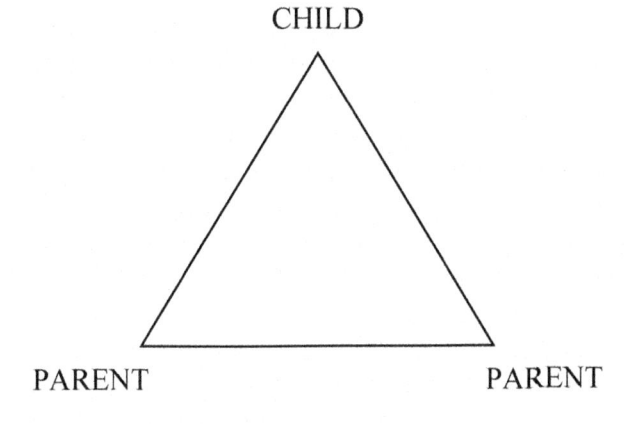

CHILD

PARENT   PARENT

This makes it easier for people to understand the concept, and helps create change in their parenting relationship. Unlike the typical family hierarchy, this image more closely parallels the dynamics in a family group. There is a strong base at the bottom, with an apex reaching for the sky. If children are told "The Sky Is The Limit," parents have an obligation to help the child reach for that goal. This is accomplished by working cooperatively, and providing the child with the necessary foundation.

Communication

The Family Triangle illustrates basic connections that must exist in a child-parent group. While all of the lines are important, in mediation, special focus is often needed on the connection between the parents. From a functional perspective, it represents communication, understanding of differences, and support of each other. It is also acknowledging that even though the romantic relationship ended, the parental relationship must continue. It is genuinely putting the needs of the child above of the wants and needs of the parents.

As shown in Figure 1, *The Family Triangle* has the child at the top with the parents as the base. As children age, they become physically bigger and heavier. Over time, their emotional weight also increases. This is especially true for families engaged in mediation. Think of a child starting their emotional journey with a pencil case and by the time they're a teenager, they may already be carrying a suitcase of emotional baggage. Parents are often left unprepared.

As the base of *The Family Triangle*, the parents remain as the support for the child; constantly trying to prop them up and help them reach their goals. The dilemma is that without functional and productive communication between the parents, there is nothing keeping the child's base points connected and secure. Over time, with lack of communication and lack of understanding, the base points slide further and further apart. Eventually, the base can no longer support the peak, and the child emotionally crashes to the ground.

Figure 2:

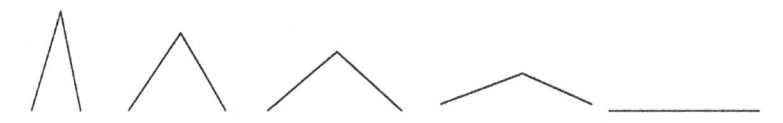

It is through this simple illustration that many parents come to a realization about their family group. To keep the base from sliding apart and the child from crashing, parents need to maintain functional and productive communication with each other. They do not need to be in constant communication, but they need to demonstrate an ability to communicate effectively to show the child they are working together in the child's best interests.

Parenting Styles

The Family Triangle can also be used to discuss healthy parenting styles, and the need for balance. Many clients express how the other parent has a different parenting style from them, and this causes great stress. The triangle allows clients to visualize the need for similarities and differences in their parenting.

It is important for parents to have some similarities in their parenting style, but they do not need to be identical. In fact, even in-tact families have parents with some differences in parenting styles. Variation is good! The slight variations in dealing with day-to-day issues help the child to adjust to variations they will encounter in the outside world. Using *The Family Triangle* demonstrates that if the styles are too similar, the base is too narrow. The structure is unstable and even though the child's emotional weight may not be as high, it takes less to emotionally knock the child over.

Figure 3:

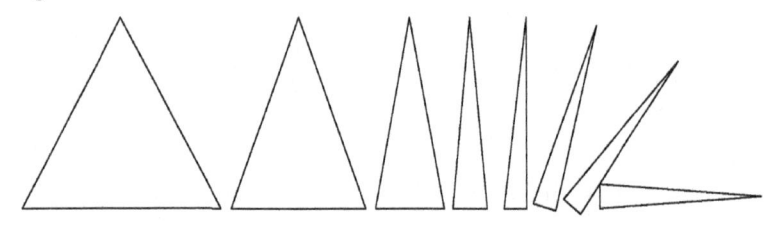

Conversely, if the parenting styles are too different, this again increases the emotional weight of the child on an unsteady base. The child then lives in a world of chaos, because the differences far outnumber the similarities. As in Figure 2, the base slips out and once again, the child emotionally crumbles to the ground.

Conclusion

Clinicians are often looking for new, intricate ways of interacting with clients. Far too often however, the processes and strategies become complicated and confusing. Sometimes, the best teaching tools are the simplest teaching tools. Clients engaged in the mediation process are often emotionally drained by the time they enter into the process. By using a simple geometric shape, the message gets through without creating further stress or confusion.

Article edited by: Dr Michael A Heintz & Nick Halmasy, HonBA, MACP

THANK YOU

I would like to thank the following people who have helped with this project on some level. Some of them proof-read early drafts, provided suggestions, or helped with topics and design. Others have helped shape me as a mediator either directly or indirectly...

- Rob Burriss
- Nick Halmasy
- Paul Hamilton
- Dr Michael Heintz
- Paul Lamain
- Carolyn Leach
- Hilary Linton
- Carolyn McAlpine
- Jared Phillips
- David Tonge
- Jess Uddenberg
- Vicky Visca

and of course, my amazing wife...

APPENDIX

Appendix A:

CONSENT TO DISCLOSE INFORMATION

I _____ of _____
　(Name of Parent/Guardian or Child over 12 Years)　　　　　　　　　(Address)

authorize _____ to release information to _____
　　　　　(Name of Agency or Person)

pertaining to:

_____ for the purpose of
(Name of Adult/Child(ren))

Child Protection Mediation and/ or Family Group Decision Making.

I understand a brief description of the service I am receiving or have sought, as well as my strengths and any worries the service provider has about me or my situation will be provided to the coordinator so that it can be shared at the family meeting. The service provider will also identify if and what resources are still available to me.

This consent will remain in effect from _____ to _____
　　　　　　　　　　　　　　　　　　　　　(Date)　　　　　　　(Date)

My signature means that:
1. I have read this consent or have had this consent read to me. I understand and agree to its contents.
2. I have been informed that I may cancel my consent by giving a written statement to the Mediator and/ or my Child Protection Worker at any time.

Signed _____ on _____ .
　　　　(Parent/Guardian or Child over 12)　　　　　　　　　(Date)

Witness _____　　_____
　　　　　　(Print Name)　　　　　　　　　　　　　(Signature)

Appendix B:

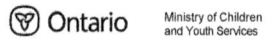

Ontario — Ministry of Children and Youth Services

Notice: Where Alternative Dispute Resolution is Proposed Under the *Child and Family Services Act*

Please fax the form to the address below:

Office of the Children's Lawyer
Ministry of the Attorney-General
393 University Avenue, 14th Floor
Toronto ON M5G 1W9
Tel: 416 314-8062
Fax: 416 314-8050
Attn.: ADR Intake Co-ordinator

Section I Child Information

Last Name	First Name	Date of Birth (yyyy/mm/dd)	Is the child a minor parent? ☐ Yes ☐ No
Last Name	First Name	Date of Birth (yyyy/mm/dd)	Is the child a minor parent? ☐ Yes ☐ No
Last Name	First Name	Date of Birth (yyyy/mm/dd)	Is the child a minor parent? ☐ Yes ☐ No
Last Name	First Name	Date of Birth (yyyy/mm/dd)	Is the child a minor parent? ☐ Yes ☐ No

Section II Contact Information

1. Children's Aid Society

Name of Agency

Name of Child Protection Worker

Address (Number and Street)		Suite/Unit/Apt.	City/Town
Province	Postal Code	Telephone Number (inc. area code) ( )	Fax Number (inc. area code) ( )
Name of Lawyer			Lawyer's Telephone Number (inc. area code) ( )

2. Parents/Caregivers

Last Name	First Name	Relationship to Child
Address (Number and Street)		Suite/Unit/Apt.
City/Town	Province	Postal Code	Telephone Number (inc. area code) ( )
Name of Lawyer		Lawyer's Telephone Number (inc. area code) ( )

Do any of the children reside at the parent/caregiver's address?
☐ Yes ☐ No If "Yes," please provide name(s) of child(ren):

0011 (11/2005)   © Queen's Printer for Ontario, 2006   Page 1 of 4   3730-0008

Last Name	First Name		Relationship to Child
Address *(Number and Street)*			Suite/Unit/Apt.
City/Town	Province	Postal Code	Telephone Number *(inc. area code)* ( )
Name of Lawyer			Lawyer's Telephone Number *(inc. area code)* ( )

Do any of the children reside at the parent/caregiver's address?
☐ Yes ☐ No   If "Yes," please provide name(s) of child(ren):

3. Other Participants, if known

Last Name	First Name		Relationship to Child
Address *(Number and Street)*			Suite/Unit/Apt.
City/Town	Province	Postal Code	Telephone Number *(inc. area code)* ( )
Name of Lawyer			Lawyer's Telephone Number *(inc. area code)* ( )

Do any of the children reside at this participant's address?
☐ Yes ☐ No   If "Yes," please provide name(s) of child(ren):

Last Name	First Name		Relationship to Child
Address *(Number and Street)*			Suite/Unit/Apt.
City/Town	Province	Postal Code	Telephone Number *(inc. area code)* ( )
Name of Lawyer			Lawyer's Telephone Number *(inc. area code)* ( )

Do any of the children reside at this participant's address?
☐ Yes ☐ No   If "Yes," please provide name(s) of child(ren):

4. Language
Does this family require services in French?
☐ Yes ☐ No

Section III   Issues Proposed for ADR

Is ADR proposed:

- in relation to a child/children who are or may be in need of protection?
  ☐ Yes ☐ No   If "Yes," proceed to Part 1 of this section.

- in relation to an openness order?
  ☐ Yes ☐ No   If "Yes," proceed to Part 2 of this section.

Part 1 Matters relating to children who are or may be in need of protection

Is there an ongoing court proceeding in relation to this matter?
☐ Yes ☐ No

Provide brief description of protection concerns

What are the issues proposed for ADR?

☐ Parent/teen conflict
☐ Expiring temporary care agreement
☐ Placement issues
☐ Terms of supervision orders
☐ Access issues
☐ Crown wardship orders/reviews
☐ Foster parents/CAS/parent issues
☐ Long term care issues
☐ Poor communication between worker and parents
☐ Length of time in care and conditions for return
☐ Other *(Please specify)*

Part 2 Matters in relation to openness orders

Please attach a copy of the openness order.

Is a
☐ variation of the openness order, or
☐ termination of the openness order

being sought?

Who has applied to vary or terminate the openness order?

Was the application brought
☐ before adoption, or
☐ after adoption?

What are the proposed issues for ADR?

Section IV Criminal Matters

Have any charges been laid in relation to this matter?
☐ Yes ☐ No

Are there any pending criminal investigations in relation to this matter?
☐ Yes ☐ No

Have criminal record checks been requested for any of the parents/caregivers/participants?
☐ Yes ☐ No

Section V ADR Process

What prescribed method of ADR is proposed?

☐ Child protection mediation
☐ Family group conferencing
☐ Aboriginal approach
☐ Other (Please specify) _____
☐ Not yet known

Has a mediator/facilitator been chosen?
☐ Yes ☐ No

Name of Mediator/Facilitator	Telephone Number (inc. area code) ( )

Section VI Optional Information

Please provide any other information that may be material to the intake process at the Office of the Children's Lawyer.
(for example: child's special needs, any issues that may impact on child's ability to communicate, any language barriers)

_____

_____

Section VII Signature

In the opinion of this worker:
☐ there is no immediate risk to the child(ren)'s safety; and
☐ the proposed participants have the capacity to participate in an ADR process.

Last Name	First Name

Position	Telephone Number (inc. area code) ( )

_____   _____
Signature   Date (yyyy/mm/dd)

Appendix C:

CONFIDENTIALITY AGREEMENT
(Mediation Intake)

1. Mediation is a voluntary process, and any participant has the right to withdraw from the process at any time.

2. The mediator was an employee of the Hastings Children's Aid Society until July 4, 2011. The mediator is no longer an employee of the Hastings Children's Aid Society and as such, does not have access to the family's child welfare history beyond what is disclosed in the mediation process.

3. The mediator will not voluntarily disclose any verbal and/ or written communication that takes place during this meeting. The following exceptions apply:
   - Disclosure for my lawyer or third party advisors;
   - Where information suggests an actual or perceived threat to human life and/ or safety (notify CAS for a child, notify Police for an adult);
   - Where ordered to do so by law;
   - Research and/ or educational purposes (non-identifying information);
   - On written consent

4. I consent to the presence of language interpreters, mediation interns and/ or assistants for the purposes of professional training. All such observers and/ or participants are also bound by the same rules of confidentiality as the mediator as outlined in Paragraph 3.

5. I shall not record the content of any mediation appointments through any means such as audio, video etc.

6. I shall not summons nor otherwise require the mediator to testify and/or produce records and/ or notes in any current or future civil proceedings.

I acknowledge that I have read the *Confidentiality Agreement* or had it read to me, and understand this agreement.

Name (Print)	Signature	Date
Name (Print)	Signature	Date
Third Party as Per Paragraph 3	Signature	Date
	Signature	Date

Appendix D:

INTAKE

Native: ☐Yes ☐No   Band: _____   Children: _____

Lawyer: ☐Yes ☐No   Name: _____   Interview Children: ☐Yes ☐No
OK to Call: ☐Yes ☐No
Court: ☐None   ☐CFSA   ☐Family   Next: _____   Restrictions: ☐Yes ☐No

History: _____
_____
_____
_____
_____
_____
_____
_____
_____
_____
_____
_____
_____
_____
_____
_____
_____
_____
_____
_____
_____
_____

MH: Past ☐   Present ☐   Subs: Past ☐   Present ☐

Adds: Past ☐   Present ☐   Tx: Yes ☐   No ☐

Strengths: _____
_____

Goals: _____
_____

Preferred Appointment Time: _____   Same Room: ☐Yes ☐No

Appendix E:

INTAKE - Worker

Court: ☐None ☐CFSA ☐ Family Next:_____ Restrictions: ☐Yes ☐ No
OCL Notified: ☐Yes   ☐ No   Assigned: ☐Yes   ☐ No

OCL Name:_____
Native: ☐Yes ☐ No Band:_____
Children: Interview Children: ☐Yes ☐ No

History:_____

_____
_____
_____
_____
_____
_____
_____
_____
_____
_____
_____
_____
_____
_____
_____
_____
_____
_____

MH: Past ☐ / Present ☐   Subs: Past ☐ / Present ☐
Adds: Past ☐ / Present ☐   Tx: Yes ☐ No ☐

Strengths:_____
_____

Goals:_____
_____

Preferred Appointment Time: Same Room: ☐Yes ☐ No

Appendix F:

AGREEMENT TO MEDIATE

This is an Agreement Between:

_____

and

_____

and

_____

and

_____

and

_____

and

_____
("the parties")

AND

"THE MEDIATOR"
(Name of Mediator)

1. The people named above want to try to settle the dispute between them through mediation with "The Mediator."

2. <u>Role of Mediator</u>
   Each person understands that the mediator does not represent any of the parties, and is not acting as a lawyer (whether

trained as one or not) for any of them. The mediator's job is to help the parties to come to an agreement which the parties think is fair and reasonable, and in the best interests of the child(ren).

3. Independent Legal Representation
The parties understand that the mediator will not give them legal advice or a legal opinion. The parties understand that they can and should speak to a lawyer about their situation, and that they can do so at any time.

4. Confidentiality
The parties agree that mediation is confidential with the following exceptions:
   a) The mediator can talk or write about the case without using identifying information for research of educational purposes;
   b) The mediator must report any suspicions that a child may be in need of protection under The Child and Family Services Act.
   c) The mediator must disclose where there are reasonable grounds to believe that there is a real or perceived threat to any person's life or physical safety.
   d) The mediator may speak to a third party where an individual consents to the disclosure of his or her own personal information.
   e) The terms of an agreement, memorandum of understanding or plan arising from the mediation can be shared with the court, and all counsel, including counsel for the child where applicable.
   f) Participants may always discuss the content of Mediation with their lawyer.

The parties agree that neither the participants nor the mediator can be subpoenaed, required to testify or called to give evidence relating to representations, statements or admissions made in the course of the mediation, or to produce or called to produce documents prepared or exchanged during the mediation in a civil proceeding.

No parties, including their lawyers, shall take any notes or recordings of any joint mediation session(s). The only exception to this rule is with respect to a lawyer representing a child when the child is not in attendance for the joint mediation session(s). Notes taken by a child's lawyer shall only contain a list of agreements reached in principle.

5. Bringing Other People into the Mediation
   The mediator may ask other people to participate in the mediation if the parties agree.

6. Disclosure of Information
   The parties agree that they will each make available any information that may help to resolve the dispute.

7. Mediation Sessions
   The mediator will schedule the time and place of the mediation sessions with the parties. The parties agree to give the mediator 24 hours notice if the session has to be cancelled.

   The mediator may meet with the parties together or individually.

8. Conclusion of Mediation
   Any party has the right to withdraw from the mediation at any time. The mediator has the right to end or suspend the mediation where continuing the process could harm or prejudice one or more of the parties or the child(ren).

   The only information the mediator will send to the parties and their lawyer(s) will be a list of any agreements in principle reached. No agreements reached in mediation are binding and it is strongly recommended that they be reviewed by each participant's counsel.

9. Further Agreements
   The parties agree that none of them will begin any court action during the course of mediation without first advising the other

party/ parties and the mediator. Any court action already started will be adjourned until the mediation ends.

The parties agree that they have read this agreement or had this agreement read to them, understand it, and agree to take part in mediation on the basis of this agreement.

_____day of _____20____

_____
Signature

_____
Signature

_____
Signature

_____
Signature

_____
Signature

_____
Signature

_____
Mediator

REFERENCES

Child and Family Services Act of 1990, R.S.O., (2016)

Heintz, M. (2012). Study outline: Version 20120122.

https://www.attorneygeneral.jus.gov.on.ca

http://www.canadacourtwatch.com

http://www.children.gov.on.ca

http://www.cpmed.ca

http://dictionary.cambridge.org

http://www.oacas.org

http://psychologytoday.com

http://www.socialworkdegreeguide.com

http://www.torontocas.ca

http://www.un.org

Landau, Barbara. (2008). Domestic violence screening and practice skills. Cooperative Solutions.

Maresca, J.A., Hall, M., & Chornenki, G.A. (2006). Child protection mediation: an introductory course. Ontario Ministry of Children and Youth Services.

Ontario Association of Children's Aid Societies (2016). Ontario Child Welfare Eligibility Spectrum (Revised).

paul@paulbrownmediation.com

CPSIA information can be obtained
at www.ICGtesting.com
Printed in the USA
LVOW03s1028080418
572687LV00005B/943/P

9 781365 889301